ALWAYS IN THE RUNNING

ALWAYS IN THE RUNNING
The Manchester United Dream Team

JIM WHITE

MAINSTREAM
PUBLISHING
EDINBURGH AND LONDON

To my mum

First published in Great Britain in 1996 by
MAINSTREAM PUBLISHING COMPANY (EDINBURGH) LTD
7 Albany Street
Edinburgh EH1 3UG

ISBN 1 85158 901 5

A catalogue record for this book is available from the British Library

Typeset in Garamond
Printed and bound in Great Britain by Butler and Tanner Ltd, Frome

CONTENTS

INTRODUCTION 7

WILLIE MORGAN Life on the Wing 15

MARTIN BUCHAN The Man Who Made Motty 35

GORDON HILL The Gordon Hill Joke Continues 49

BRYAN ROBSON Thirteen Years and Won the Lot 63

NORMAN WHITESIDE Feet First 79

PAUL MCGRATH Ooh, Aah, Mine's a Jar 93

MARK HUGHES Not a Great Goal-Scorer, Apparently 107

STEVE BRUCE Captain Responsible 121

RYAN GIGGS Top Snog 131

PETER SCHMEICHEL You Know What They Say
  about Big Hands 145

ERIC CANTONA The Leader of Our Football Team 155

ALEX FERGUSON The Boss 171

ACKNOWLEDGEMENTS

Without a certain dozen men, there would have been no book here, so thanks to them for giving me such pleasure over the years. Especially, though, I'm grateful to Willie Morgan, Martin Buchan, Gordon Hill, Norman Whiteside, Mark Hughes, Bryan Robson, Steve Bruce, Ryan Giggs and Alex Ferguson for wasting their time talking to me. Eric, of course, doesn't need to communicate with anything other than his feet. I'm particularly indebted for help to the United sages: Richard Kurt, Andy Mitten, Jim Phelan for snaps (don't forget to buy the George Best album, folks) and the wonderful Michael Crick, with his Bodlein library of red tomes. And thanks to Ian Ridley, Henry Winter and Patrick Barclay for supplying opinions which appear to have come out as my own.

Thanks, too, to John Whiston, Stephen Franklin and Bridget Bosely ('that kid'll go far') for tolerating me and then letting me loose on the transcripts; to Sam Anthony who stopped the whole thing degenerating into hagiography; to Pete Frame for being a guru; to all at Mainstream for having the idea; to Chris and Karen for the bed and the griddled tuna steak; and to the wonderful Eugen, the smooth oil in the machinery. Oh, and to Cat: top man in her field.

And most of all thanks to Arabella for tolerating the madness: and still no Aga.

INTRODUCTION

The mini cab firm local to my house appears to require three things of its employees: that they cannot drive, do not know their way around London and cannot speak English. 'Ah, King's Cross, what is?' one of their lads once asked me. 'Is in London?'

But one driver who picked me up early one morning in February 1996 had no problems, he spoke the one true international language. As I opened the front door of my house, he stood on the doorstep gesticulating in a thumbs-aloft manner at the little dangly red shirt hanging by a suction pad from my son's bedroom window.

'Ah, yes,' he said, cheery at 5.30 a.m. 'Manchester United, very good. Yes, best team in world.'

He supported them, then?

'Ah yes, Manchester United, very good. Yes, best team in world.'

And why did he support them? I asked.

'Ah yes, Manchester United, very good. Yes, best team in world.'

So, where, I wondered, did he come from?

'The Sudan,' he said.

When I later told that story to a colleague who maintains an interest in Manchester City, I meant it to serve as an example of the difference in scale between our respective teams, to point out that the bars of downtown Mogadishu echo to discussions of the merits of Butt and Beckham rather than Lomas and Summerbee, to indicate that some of us dealt with an international commodity, while others engaged in an activity barely known outside Moss Side. But he thought it was the funniest thing he'd heard since news of the appointment of Alan Ball. 'The bloke comes from Sudan,' was his rib-tickled analysis. 'Typical United supporter, then.'

I should have known. This is the thing you have to put up with as a United supporter: that somehow the club's very popularity across the globe taints your commitment. The fact that seven-year-olds in Portsmouth, Penrith and Potters Bar pester their parents to spend much of the family income on items in man-made fabric advertised in the Megastore Mail Order catalogue is taken as proof positive that to follow the boys of Man United is to grab the easy option, that to pledge allegiance to the reds is to clamber aboard a monolithic bandwagon occupied solely by the clueless. The pop group Catatonia issued a tour T-shirt last spring which said it all. A parody of the United jersey, it had on the back a big number seven and across the shoulders the word Catatonia. And on the front, where the sponsors' logo is, instead of Sharp it read Sheep.

It is something you experience at every ground where you go to watch United play these days: Gooners from Banbury and Basingstoke filling Highbury with the taunting boast that they support their local team; Norwegians in black and white face paint at St James's Park mocking that 'you don't come from Manchester'; Hampshire Whites at Elland Road attesting that they hate Cockney reds.

And the burgeoning smart alec wing of footie humour find this a particularly fecund furrow to plough. For *When Saturday Comes*, for Skinner and Baddiel, for *Total Football* magazine, true football support is about standing with not many others on freezing terraces at bad grounds watching your team from a provincial town, at present languishing in the lower reaches of the Football League, lose. And then laughing about the expanse of your useless centre-forward's backside ten years later. It's about finding solace in the face of adversity. An English thing, it's about drawing pleasure from self-inflicted pain.

Thus to support Manchester United and to spend your time revelling in glorious, life-enhancing football in the company of a spiritual diaspora spread across the globe is characterised as a failure of understanding of the true nature of the game, it is to mistake the ersatz for the genuine, to be a fake. As Nick Hancock said of Angus Deayton when he guested on *Room 101*: he's not a football fan, he supports Man U.

Moreover, in these days of boardroom greed, commercialisation and the remorseless drive of football's businessmen to remove the coinage from spectators' pockets – skills at which Manchester United plc are peerless – to be a red is assumed to be a party to everything that is wrong with the game.

Such thinking is obviously what motivated the QPR fan on Shepherd's Bush station in March 1996 who, on hearing my seven-year-old son's friend explain that he had never been to Old Trafford, turned on our party and angrily suggested we were 'typical United fans'; or the Bolton supporter I saw in January 1996 standing on a footbridge near Burnden Park with his arms outstretched, doing wobbly aircraft impressions at cars with United pennants passing underneath, occasionally lobbing stones at them with a cry of 'fucking Munichs'; or the Chelsea follower on the tube to Wembley in May 1994 who smacked me on the side of the head and then, when a 50-year-old bloke told him to steady on, this was the Cup final after all, said 'so what, you're scum' and proceeded to nut him. There is no doubting one thing these days: if you don't love United, you hate them.

The standard Old Trafford response to the new hatred is to blame envy. And, in truth, there is a lot to be envious about out there among the lower orders. United should, long ago, have been referred to the Monopolies Commission for their greedy carve-up of domestic trophies and their even greedier colonisation of the football merchandise business. At Old Trafford, what constitutes failure is the 1994–95 season when the club was but two blinding saves from the double. That and the fact profits trebled rather than quadrupled as predicted.

But nonetheless, however comforting success is (very comforting, since you ask), such relentless assault from our enemies has made me over the past couple of years challenge my own convictions. What is it that makes me a United fan? Do I really suffer from insufficiently advanced levels of discernment? Why do I invest so much, both emotionally and financially, in following a club which many of my friends and colleagues appear to regard as Satan's earthly representative? Also, how do you excuse Roy Keane?

The reasons are many. It is something to do with the historical accident of time and place. When I was eight, and forming allegiances in a playground five miles from Old Trafford and not much more from Maine Road, we could choose between the Champions of England and the Champions of Europe. I went (typical United fan) for the greater glory. And I was stuck with it, even when City made a much better fist of things in my early adolescence.

It is something to do with the sight and sound of 15,000 in the Stretford End the first time I stood on its fringes chanting 'you-gonna-get-your-fuckin-eads-kicked-in' at the little knot of opposition spectators at the other end of the ground and me thinking, blimey.

It is something, too, to do with a regionalist identity. When I was at university and later at work away from Manchester, supporting United acted as a statement of where I came from, what I valued, who I was. Granted, not so much use in these days of global red domination ('what, a United fan from Manchester, that's unusual, tee hee') but it served me well back then.

It is something also to do with my fellow fans I have got to know over the years through our shared infatuation; people who, with one or two exceptions, I count as friends. All those things, though, could equally obtain for the life-long Arbroath, Aston Villa or Plymouth Argyle supporter. But there is one thing about following United that sets you apart from almost all other supporters: the players.

Football allegiance involves levels of hero worship that would, in most other contexts, be regarded as dangerously obeisant. Grown men like films, pop music and fashion, but they would never spend hours in the pub with a couple of mates constructing their perfect cast list for a Martin Scorsese thriller; they wouldn't ritually go to watch the same band play the G-Mex centre every Saturday; they wouldn't subscribe to an otherwise intolerable newspaper every Wednesday simply to keep up with developments in the fantasy designers' league (Paul Smith's new autumn collection gets three points for a tidy assist in the trouser area). Yet because we have all dabbled in the game, and love playing it more than anything, to witness those who can master it in a way which we only attain during the hours of midnight and 7 a.m. is to see what we would like to be. A survey of college athletes in America before the last Olympics revealed that if offered a pill which would guarantee them a gold medal, but also kill them painfully and horribly by the age of 30, 90 per cent said they would take it. Offer the same pill to a fan to play for United and take-up would be the full 100.

Such hero worship, it seems to me, can only be reconcilable to our personal pride if it attaches itself to the best. And at Old Trafford over three decades of observing I have seen a level of excellence bettered domestically by no one except Liverpool. I have seen players prodigiously endowed with gifts of balance and brain, fleet-footedness and speed of thought. I've also seen Arnie Sidebottom, Tommy Jackson and Alex Forsyth, but that's another story.

Skill, application and intelligence are not traits unique to Manchester United players. But what the greats of Old Trafford possess in more abundance than almost all the rest is a strength of character and a mental resilience to sustain them through the critical core of their employment: being a Manchester United player.

There was a fantastic photograph of David Beckham taken towards the end of the 1996 FA Cup final. He was snapped addressing the ball at a corner. Behind him is banked the Wembley crowd in their thousands, every eye staring at him, every one of them mentally projecting on him their aspirations for that moment: 'make this one count, son' or 'cock it up, you Manc twat'. Via the television camera over his left shoulder, a billion other eyes were invited to set an exam for his mental capabilities; back home in Sudan, my cabbie's family were doubtless watching, through Beckham connected to their son, imagining him glued to that same moment in exile in a dark and dangerous place (the London Borough of Islington). Under the pressure of delivering a corner to my mates during a park game, I've crumbled and stubbed it wide. But under a pressure unimaginable to us, Beckham didn't appear concerned. He arced the ball along a sweet parabola into the bad place; James, the Liverpool goalkeeper, fluffing his exam, swatted meekly at it and diverted it into the path of Eric Cantona; and the man who has faced a few pressures of his own making over the years steadied himself, balanced, applied himself to the ball and duly sent it past half a dozen opponents into the net.

To be a Manchester United player, you have to be able to do what Beckham did. Many who have worn the red (and the black, white, blue, yellow, green and Uncle Tom Cobley) haven't managed it. Ted MacDougall, Terry Gibson, Peter Davenport, Garry Birtles and, let's be honest, Andy Cole, comprehensively failed to reproduce the form they showed elsewhere. Not because their skill evaporated at Old Trafford's gates, but because the expectation engendered by us fans – the arrogant assumption that we deserve only the best available – overwhelmed them. The thought of what lay ahead made poor Alan Brazil throw up before every game; Gordon McQueen too, and he had far less to be worried about. Ask any player and they'll tell you, the warmest place in Old Trafford just before a match is always the seat of the dressing-room lavs.

To be a red hero requires a particular blend of skill, spirit and resilience. Ray Wilkins once told me that, in his early days at United, he was booed off the pitch at Old Trafford by those who felt he wasn't playing like a man who cost the club a British record. 'And they were right,' he said, 'I wasn't.' The noise and the faces of that awful trudge off the field still come back to him, fresh and vivid and hurtful: 'you don't forget that,' he said. 'It cuts you deep.'

But Wilkins had the reserves to overcome self-pity and play his way into our affections: in his last season in 1984, before he was scandalously let go to Milan, he played every game and in every game he was magnificent. And when he came back to Old Trafford as manager of QPR, dapper and neat, the floodlight bouncing off his hair-free pate, instead of there being a chorus of boos, the superstructure of the new north stand was put in danger by the volume of the welcome he received.

Over the years we have been fortunate in the wealth of players like him. This book is about 11 of the men most gifted, plus a manager substantial enough to cope with the altogether more sizeable prerequisites of running a place like Old Trafford.

The choice was not an easy one. Gordon Hill told me that one game, early on in his United career, he scored a belter of a goal, a screamer from outside the box hit on the volley from a corner. He said that as he trotted back for the kick-off, at that moment he felt accepted. Not so much by the management leaping around in the dug-out just out of eye-shot, not so much by the crowd roaring their welcomes around him, but by the turf itself. The Old Trafford pitch, haunted by the ghosts of a thousand great performances, told him he was all right, son.

And United have more ghosts than most: Johnny Carey, Charlie Mitten, the Busby Babes. But none of them figure here in this book. The trouble with ghosts is, we have to rely on others' judgements of their merits. I decided in making my choice of the United Dream Team that I would restrict inclusion to those I had seen in action in the flesh. It had to be that way, because if you include, as you must, Duncan Edwards in a list of unequivocally the all-time greatest United players, why not Billy Meredith, whose skills no one alive today has witnessed, but who legend tells us was the best? And if Billy Meredith, why not James Brown, a Scotsman signed at sea who scored for the USA in the 1930 World Cup semi-final? Or Frank Barson, a blacksmith by trade, who knocked out a Manchester City player cold with one blow during the 1926 FA Cup semi-final? Or Caesar Augustus Llewelyn Jenkins, 15 stone of intimidation, who used to waddle around for the reds when they were the green and yellows of Newton Heath at the turn of the century and who, even if he was no good, should be in anyone's side on grounds of top nomenclature.

The trouble is, by dint of a dad who didn't get the plot at all (when I was nine and first developing signs of football insanity, he took me to watch Altrincham in the Cheshire League, when just down the road the greatest party in England was being held every fortnight) and a mum who assumed going to Old Trafford entailed returning home with a dart through the bridge of the nose, I didn't get to see the reds until I was 14 and could make my own choices. By that time Bobby Charlton had retired, George Best self-destructed and Denis Law was wearing blue, apologetically back-heeling a critical goal at the Scoreboard End and then endearing himself to reds everywhere by refusing his team-mates' invitation to celebrate. So none of them can make the cut. Nor can Nobby Stiles, even though I went to see the film *Goal* about the 1966 World Cup when it first came out and perfected the Nobby dance, the one where he jigged round Wembley with the Jules Rimet trophy on his head. Pat Crerand can't be in there, either, even though he was a great player and now as a radio analyser shows a lack of rancour, a spirit and an enthusiasm about the present-day players sad old fools like Fred 'it were not like that in my day' Truman ought to learn from. Nor can Albert Quixall, Elvis-quiffed forward in the early '60s, be picked. Shame; his dressing-room practical jokes involving turds would have merited a few paragraphs of Freudian examination (wrapping them up in fancy paper and leaving them on a newcomer's place in the dressing-room before a match, marked with a note suggesting the contents were from a particularly ardent female admirer, was number one in the Quixall shit parade).

Still, 22 years watching the reds hasn't restricted the field greatly. Here are some that didn't make the cut: Stepney, Bailey, Albiston, Irwin, Moran, McQueen, Pallister, the Neville brothers, McIlroy, Macari, Wilkins, Ince, Moses, Keane, Butt, Coppell, Kanchelskis, McClair, Pearson, Jordan, Sharpe, Strachan, Scholes. Clayton Blackmore, too, worthy of consideration for one fact alone: he is the only player in United history to have worn every number on his back from 2 to 11.

Those who did make the team, though, had something more about them even than that spectacular list of talent. They are my heroes, men whose bearing and character, as well as skill and enterprise, elevate them from among their peers; men who had a spark, men who had an edge, men who epitomise what it is we fans think of as United.

Thus it is a team without full-backs. Full-backs aren't heroes; they are dependable and trustworthy; players you don't really notice are there. I should know: I'm a full-back. Shorn of defensive reliability, with a glut of fancy-dan wingers, it is a recklessly attacking team, playing a mad 3–4–3 formation and it reads: Peter Schmeichel; Martin Buchan, Steve Bruce, Paul McGrath; Willie Morgan, Norman Whiteside, Bryan Robson, Ryan Giggs; Eric Cantona, Mark Hughes, Gordon Hill.

Maybe it is not the greatest team ever to play for United, but it would certainly be the best company in the bar afterwards. During my time I have seen teams managed by Tommy Docherty, Dave Sexton, Ron Atkinson and Alex Ferguson. There is no argument who will be in charge of this team, then. Alex Ferguson would relish the challenge, as he would term it, of corralling this lot.

I haven't seen the Sudanese cabbie since that bleak February day, incidentally. If I do again, I probably won't canvass his opinion as to who should be in the team. Back then, as we span through the dark, cold, empty streets of early-morning London, I did what you always do when you meet a fellow believer: I asked him who his all-time favourite United player was. He looked into the rear view mirror, stuck up his thumb and grinned. 'Mickey Thomas,' he said.

The question must have lost something in the translation.

LIFE ON THE WING

Willie Morgan. Life began: 28.8.68

The 1996 FA Cup final didn't deserve a goal like that. A turgid procession of nerves and stifled enterprise, the game between Manchester United and Liverpool, the top bollocks of English football, was so bad you never thought a goal was coming. By the 83rd minute I was grateful that the £55 I had paid for a Wembley seat afforded a perfect view of a pillar, which blocked off half of the centre circle from view, thus obscuring many of the scuffed passes and bouts of head tennis which comprised the 110th final. On the 84th minute, I turned to my mate Alistair sitting next to me and said that if anyone was going to score, it would be a scramble, a stubbed shot, a dispute over whether the ball really had trickled over the line. David May, I reckoned, would get it. And it could come at either end.

Instead Eric Cantona intervened. From the edge of the box in the 85th minute of the snooze-fest, he delivered a goal of beauty and of perfection; a shot which stung past six Liverpool defenders and a statuesque, grinning David May. It was a goal that wasn't just about winning a Cup final and sealing a double (a double double, to remind anyone reading this in Liverpool), though. It was a goal full of implication. That muggy May afternoon, as he swung his right foot, Eric Cantona issued a manifesto; a statement of intent to prove to all the doubters and all the critics who he was and what he was capable of producing. This was the goal that confirmed the second coming.

And as I jumped out of my Wembley seat, yelping monosyllables of triumph into the north London sky, a sense of *déjà vu* washed over

15

me. I had, I remembered, seen a goal like that before; a goal of resonance and deliberation, a goal pregnant with meaning. Not only that, it was one of the first goals I had ever seen at Old Trafford. It was a goal that was to have a profound effect on me: it was the goal that changed my hair style.

You can tell what kind of place Manchester Grammar School is by the front drive. Arrow-straight and unyielding, it is an engineering metaphor for the purpose of the institution at its top. Everyone who enters MGS's gates is shoved on a relentless trajectory towards the ultimate goal: becoming a lawyer. The thirteenth of November 1974 was a day like any other at the school, a day that began with double Latin and ended with quadruple Maths, a typical day, a day of head down and graft. But the moment it was over and the bell sounded, I was off, legging it up the drive with my mate Jon to start preparations for an encounter with the real world.

Once we got home, off came the charcoal grey trousers, the blazer with the light blue owl on the breast pocket, the blue striped tie, folded time and again in the fashion of the day until it sat like a thick ball on the collar. On went the brushed denim strides with flares so big that if you walked carefully, they would conceal the fat toes of your stack-heeled brogues. On went the jumbo-collared cream shirt with the brown Homepride bakers motif repeated across the fabric. On went the beige and chocolate acrylic zip-up cardigan as favoured by Starsky (or was it Hutch?) on the telly. Around the neck was knotted a black acrylic scarf with red and white stripes and on to each wrist were tied two drapes of acrylic silk-like material, each decorated with the legend 'Manchester United: Cock of the North'. A match carelessly lit at that moment would have proved tricky. One glance in the mirror, though, confirmed what we suspected: we were the Clark Kents of Altrincham; no more Mr Swat, now we were Superfly.

In 1974, to get into the Stretford Paddock, the non-contributory part of the Stretford End, required more than the right costume, however. Even though United were in the second division at the time, it required queueing – lots of it – and a sum in your pocket not unadjacent to 40p for the junior entry fee. Wary of the queues, we got there an hour earlier than necessary, sighed with relief as we clacked through the turnstiles, bought our programme and took up our positions for the League Cup fourth-round game between United and Burnley.

What we saw that night was well worth 40p of anyone's money. United, in a harbinger of what was to come, were, that year, for one season only, wearing a new creation by Umbro. A deep scarlet polo shirt, with a plain white collar, the tips of which, in the style of the time, grazed the nipples; half-length white shorts unsullied by detail or design; black socks with a red top panel cut by a thin white line (Lou Macari used to fold his, out of superstition, so that the white stripe was hidden): it was the best kit United have ever worn. And in it, though they should have been humbled by relegation the previous season, the players looked cocky, swaggering, the bee's knees.

None more so than Willie Morgan. Midway through the second half, United's winger picked up a clearance from a corner midway between the centre circle and the Burnley box. Casually taking two paces forward, Morgan chipped the ball from 30 yards with all the precision of Tom Watson stroking a nine-iron pitch on to the 18th at Augusta. It arced into the top corner of the goal, precisely bisecting the space between the goalkeeper and a full-back, prosaic in white round-necked shirt, who was alleged to be minding the post. It was a stupendous goal, a corker, as good as any scored on the ground. But instead of galloping on an adrenalin-fired belt of celebration round the pitch, Morgan acknowledged his wonder by standing still, one arm raised, chewing nonchalantly on his gum, staring fixedly at the dug-out, until he was buried under a pyramid of smiley colleagues. We were not to know it on the terraces, but there was real feeling in that stare, real meaning in his lack of celebration; a point, we had no way of realising, was being made. All we thought at the time was that his behaviour confirmed what we had already suspected: Willie Morgan was cool.

A week later I had my hair cut just like his. Long tresses curled under at the back, a shorter section staggered in steps up the sides, a bouffant parted slightly to the side on top. I was soon to discover a style like this was no small commitment, it took hours of precision work with electrical appliances to retain its geometry. A stroll into the Mancunian breeze and it was gone, fluffed down like a melting meringue. Yet he played football every week in his.

Twenty-one years later, I was making a television documentary charting the Manchester United 'family tree' and set off to

Altrincham, with a camera crew, to interview Willie. We arrived at his imposing pile on the fringes of the town – the place he bought when he was a United player, wisely sinking his hard-earned cash into bricks and mortar instead of flash motors – parked on the gravel sweep of a drive, and rang the doorbell. His daughter let us into the house and suggested we might like to film the interview in one of three expansive reception rooms. Sam, the programme's director, wanted to move the furniture around, to make better use of natural light, and dispatched me, as the spare part, to seek the owner's permission. No one was around in the hall or the kitchen; no one was in the front room with its display case full of international caps and the portrait of Matt Busby over the fireplace. No one was in the third reception room where a collection of Elvis Presley porcelain covered one wall and a picture of Willie with Howard Keel and Johnny Mathis, snapped after a round of golf, stood sentry by the door. So I followed a whirring noise which was emanating from a small back closet. And there, pushing open the door, I found Willie himself. He was blow-drying his hair, a barnet which, save its new silver colouring, was identical in length and style to that night in 1975.

Willie Morgan was Matt Busby's last signing for Manchester United. But he was not the first William Morgan to play for the reds: Billy Morgan was an indomitable half-back at the turn of the century, a player known as 'the India rubber doll' for his ability to bounce back from a tackle. This Morgan, though, came from that rich seam of tricky Scottish ball-players, the one that produced Jim Baxter, Jimmy Johnson, Archie Gemmill and a hundred others, the one that the Scots fondly assumed would never be exhausted . . . but was. Pigeon-toed and bow-legged, he was a dribbler, shoulders hunched over the ball, elbows cocked like a gunslinger's, wrists hovering over his hips, eyes darting, his job to run full-backs to distraction. This is what we used to chant when he got the ball:

When Willie comes on to the field
Dressed in red and white
All the fans lift up their hands
And shout with all their might
Forget your Bells and Francis Lees
Can you hear them calling

Hey, hey clear the way, here comes Willie Morgan
Willie, Willie Morgan, Willie Morgan on the wing.

Well, actually, most of us only knew the last line.

When he was 15 every club in Scotland and most in England wanted the young wizard from the mining village of Sauchie, near Alloa. But Morgan chose Burnley because, on his trip round the clubs to see which one he preferred, he had got injured there and they were kind to him. That and the fact they were league champions at the time. It broke his father's heart, he says, that he never went to Celtic.

In 1963 after John Connelly moved to Old Trafford, the 19-year-old Morgan took over his place on Burnley's right flank. Soon the big clubs were sniffing. By the summer of 1968, Morgan was in contractual dispute with Burnley's owner, Bob Lord, whom he never got on with. Lord thought he'd better cash in on the latest product from his then enviable youth production line, and the boy, his apprenticeship complete, was put up for sale. Celtic came in for him, but his father's hopes were to come to nothing again. The moment the European champions showed an interest there was only one employer for him. Twenty-three years old, top banana at Burnley and the bloke every girl in East Lancashire dribbled over, Morgan had ideas of his own value. But when Matt Busby walked into the hotel room where Morgan was talking things over with United's assistant manager, Jimmy Murphy, all thought of negotiation went out the window. 'So you'd like to play for us, son?' Busby said. 'Good.'

'And that was it,' Morgan remembered. 'I couldn't even look at him, honestly, my head just wouldn't lift up. I just sat there like a little kid: "Yes, sir. No sir." I went home and my wife said: "So how much is he paying you?" And I said: "I've no idea." I was going back the next day and she said to me, "Well, find out." So I went in to see Matt and he showed me the contract and I signed and that was it; I still didn't ask. I joined Man United for a record fee without ever knowing how much I was going to get.' He cost £118,000. He found out the first time he opened his pay packet, negotiation or no negotiation, that Busby had looked after him.

Morgan made his debut on 28 August 1968, against Spurs at Old Trafford. The team that day was as follows: Stepney, Brennan, Dunne, Fitzpatrick, Stiles, Sadler, Morgan, Kidd, Charlton, Law,

Best. United won 3–1; Fitzpatrick got two and Beal gifted an own goal; the crowd was 62,649. He thought, as he strode off the pitch that afternoon, that he was made.

If Morgan was immediately taken by Busby, the feeling was mutual. They became firm friends, their families holidaying together and the pair regularly playing golf – a game Morgan had first discovered at Burnley, he says, 'on an afternoon the racing was cancelled'.

'Matt had such incredible presence, an aura,' Morgan recalled, as he sat on the sofa of his front room, occasionally looking up at his portrait of the old man, all paternal above the fireplace. 'There was something about him; he never raised his voice yet he commanded total respect. In all my time I never heard a player swear in front of Matt, and, I assure you, with footballers that is an incredible feat. There were no rules and no laying down the law; you just didn't misbehave with Matt.

'I remember, really early on, we had to be at the ground for 10 a.m. to catch the coach to Sheffield for an away game, and Pat Crerand asked me to pick him up from his house in Sale. Now Pat's not the most organised of guys, and when I get to his house, it's all curtained up, no sign of anyone. I'm knocking at the door, and there's no answer, so I'm thinking, Oh God! Then this head sticks out the top window, hair all over, and it's Pat, and he says: "Oh, Willie, come on in." And I'm saying, "Pat, you seen the time," and he's still not dressed. And he says: "You want a cup of tea?" Then it's: "Hey, Willie, I've got some new records, you want to hear them?" And I'm bricking it, I mean bricking it, that we're going to be late.

'Eventually I get him in the car, and we arrive at the meeting place and everyone's there, in the coach, waiting. And Matt's at the front of the coach in his usual place, and I was sweating, my bottle's gone completely, so I race over and say "I'm very, very sorry" to the gaffer and he just nodded his head. Then when we arrive at Sheffield, Matt takes me by the elbow and says: "William, a word." And I think, "Oh God, here we go." And you know what he says? "William, don't be picking up Patrick again."'

It was some side Morgan joined, and he loved it. United beat QPR 8–1 soon after he arrived; Best got two, Law got two and Morgan bettered them with three, including a dribble from his own half, mazing through much of the QPR defence to score the goal he considers his finest. In the spring of his first season, he played in the European Cup semi-final against Milan, and was denied a chance of getting into the final by a bizarre refereeing decision which ruled out a legitimate Law goal. He played in the World Club Championship, the infamous battle against Estudiantes, and remains to this day the only British player ever to score in that competition. There was just one question worrying him: would the trophy cabinet back home be big enough for the medals he was going to win?

By the autumn of 1969, Morgan's red honeymoon was over. Busby retired, became general manager and Wilf McGuinness took over as coach. Under McGuinness, Morgan only rarely tasted the glamour he had signed up for. In 1970 he was involved in another epic semi-final, this time in the FA Cup against Leeds. He has a photograph of that game on the wall of his house. It shows him emerging from the tunnel at Hillsborough, about to run through a gauntlet of girl pipers, a ball under his arm, toes pointing inwards, a look on his face which suggests he cannot be beaten. But he was. After two replays, Leeds got to Wembley, as they did frequently in the '70s. No one blamed Morgan, though. His crowd-pleasing jinks won him supporters' player of the year in 1970, a year when Best was in his prime.

McGuinness, on the other hand, was blamed. At 32, a contemporary of several and younger than a couple, he was not ready to cope with the strength of personality in that United dressing-room: Crerand, Law, Stiles, Charlton and cocky little Willie. He tried to introduce new coaching methods, the blackboard, the manual, tougher training. The boys in the dressing-room, they had won everything, under a manager they considered peerless; they thought altogether it was best to stick to the Busby way. 'I thought,' George Best says of the McGuinness approach, 'by then I probably knew how to play football.'

McGuinness thought they were all undermining his authority; he watched them off playing golf with Busby and he thought they were laughing at him behind his back, telling on him to the big man. He wasn't far from the truth. If Busby remained The Boss to his boys, what was McGuinness? 'Little Boss.'

As Morgan remembers it, McGuinness was never up to the job. 'He's a lovely fella, now, Wilf,' said Morgan. 'But he'll admit he's changed. Back then he was very, very childish, immature. He was a big one for the blackboard. I think we drew one once, but I don't ever remember winning a game on a blackboard.'

The lack of respect was mutual, incidentally. McGuinness reckoned Morgan spent too much time 'dribbling up his own arse'. But Morgan tells a story which seems to sum up Little Boss's man-management deficiencies and the way in which his attempts to exert his authority backfired so badly. It concerns a day training at the Cliff when the rain was slanting, and the mud ankle deep. Bobby Charlton had been allowed to change early – he had a business appointment – but McGuinness suddenly decided he was unhappy with the team's attitude to training. Instead of being held inside the dressing-room as usual, the team talk would be held in the middle of the pitch, he announced. Word was sent to Charlton, in the dressing-room, to come over and join them, and he tiptoed in his smart shoes through the deluge, across to where the team was gathering, a tide-mark of mud advancing up his suit trousers.

'It's horrible by now,' Morgan told me, smiling at the memory, 'so Bobby's pulled up the collar on his coat against the wind and he's put his hands in the pockets of his suit. Now Wilf has this rule, anyone caught with their hands in pockets during training, ten press ups. So Wilf spots him and says, "right, Charlton, ten press ups." And Bobby goes, "you're joking." And Wilf says, "do 'em now, else it's 20." So Bobby gets down in the mud and does 10 press ups and gets mud all over his suit. Now of course, all the rest of us, we all thought this was hilarious. But it wasn't long after that, as I recall, that Wilf got the sack.'

Indeed the incident soured relations in the dressing-room for some time. When Alex Stepney wrote about it in his autobiography, Charlton and McGuinness threatened him with a libel suit unless he withdrew it, so he did. Twenty-six years on, McGuinness, relaxed into his role as after-dinner speaker and Old Trafford buffoon ('I think I caused a bit of a rick once when I dropped Bobby Charlton and Denis Law for the same game and it made such a stink I thought I must've dropped the atom bomb' is his favourite line), now admits it happened. But he has post-rationalised it as a bit of a laugh, a giggle which summed up the *esprit de corps* at the time. Charlton prefers to forget it ever took place.

When McGuinness departed, Busby resumed duties as team manager again in December 1970 for the rest of the season, a term in which Morgan again won supporters' player of the year. But his mentor finally departed in the spring of 1971, to be replaced by Frank O'Farrell, a manager Morgan calls 'Father Frank', the studious, quiet, undemonstrative former Leicester boss.

Or rather, O'Farrell felt Busby didn't finally depart. As O'Farrell struggled to contain a wilful, declining team, whose dynamic core, George Best, was rapidly going off kilter, he wilted in the old man's shadow. He constantly worried himself that Busby, now a club director, was always around, pulling strings, stopping him making the signings he wanted to make (David Nish was one, apparently, as was Colin Todd). He thought The Boss was too ready to listen to gossip on the golf course about his deficiencies. Gossip, he thought, mainly instigated by Morgan – which is a charge Morgan denies.

'We never talked about anything on the golf course, other than golf,' Morgan told me. 'All that stuff about us telling tales to Matt, it's not true. Believe it or not, the main thing we talked about was whether he was going to make that three-foot putt or not.'

Nevertheless, in the autumn of 1972 as United were flirting dangerously with relegation, Busby did sound out his regular partner during a round at Mottram Hall golf course about one thing. What did young William think of the present Scotland manager, a man he had worked with during the mini-World Cup tournament held in Brazil that summer? Did he think he might, for instance, make a good manager of Manchester United?

Morgan was unstinting in his praise: just the man for the job, was about the sum of his advice. Thus, soon afterwards, Frank O'Farrell was paid off, though not before Thomas Henderson Docherty had accepted an offer of his job to become Manchester United manager. 'I got him the job,' said Morgan, shaking his head wryly at the thought. 'And when he first came he was a breath of fresh air after Frank. Very outgoing, very positive. He was wonderful. I think his attitude alone saved us from relegation that year.'

Much of Docherty's drive when he arrived at Old Trafford was directed at removing what he characterised as the cancer at the club. He had heard about how player power had destroyed McGuinness and O'Farrell, and determined it wasn't going to happen to him. In his mind, if he was going to survive in the most difficult post in British club football, he would have to build a team loyal only to him. And that meant an end to the old guard. Almost from the moment he took over, Docherty declared war on the Busbyites, setting about them with all the ruthlessness of an EC slaughterman. Within a year of Docherty arriving at Old Trafford, of the team Morgan had first played in, only he and Alex Stepney survived; the rest had all been culled, replaced by men who could not stop the club's perilous decline. The Morgan medal collection was put on ice.

One thing, though, with Best self-destructing, Foulkes, Crerand and Charlton retiring, Stiles, Dunne, Sadler and Kidd being dispatched elsewhere and Law, or to give him his full title, King Denis of Old Trafford, being deposed and sent into the harshest of exiles at Maine Road, was that Morgan became the centre of attention in the early days of Doc's United.

'At first you couldn't compete with Bestie; you know the press he got,' Morgan told me. 'It was impossible to take press off Bestie. Then when he left all of a sudden, it's "eh, Willie, you're a great player." And I thought: "eh, nothing's changed here, you know."'

Indeed, Docherty soon made Morgan team captain, something that suprised him as he thought George Graham [yup, that George Graham], his fellow Scot with an interest in sharp suits and luxuriant hair, was captain. 'Docherty came up to me one day after training and he said Old Smoothy [Graham] didn't really want to be captain any more, that the responsibility was getting to his play, and he wanted me to be it,' Morgan recalled. 'I said, that's great, an honour, as long as that's all right by George, because he was my friend. And Docherty says: "I told you, he doesn't want it any more." So the match that Saturday, George goes to pick up the ball, and Docherty says: "What you doing?" And George says: "I'm going to lead the boys out, boss." And Docherty says: "No you're not, Morgan is, he's skipper now," and he grabs the ball off George and chucks it at me.

'Well, after the game George isn't speaking to me. And this goes on in training the next week. After a few days, I confront him. I says: "What's all this?" And he says: "You know what it's about." "What?" "You and your pal, you've cut me up." It turns out Docherty has told him that I've been bugging him for the captaincy for months, telling him I don't rate George and how he's no good, and how he's giving me the captaincy to shut me up and he hopes George understands. I thought: "This is incredible." I couldn't work it out.'

It wasn't the skipper's fault – he was mentioned in dispatches for busting a gut in United's cause from his new central midfield position – but at the end of the 1973–74 season United were relegated. The problem was, they couldn't score: the defence, the leaky problem of the previous couple of years, had been shored, but the attack, once the pride of Manchester, no longer contained Best, Law or even Storey-Moore. It had forgotten what a net was; half-way through the season Stepney, drafted in as penalty-taker, was joint leading scorer – with two goals.

The reds were helped on their way downwards by poor old deposed King Denis, the new blue, reluctantly playing for City in the Manchester derby in April 1974. Towards the end of a goalless game, trying to get out of the way of a pass from Francis Lee in the United penalty area, Denis instead back-heeled the ball artfully past Alex Stepney. It was a moment of purest hubris: the man brutally, it was to turn out, discarded by United, easing the stiletto into the soft spot between the top of the spine and the base of the neck. Not that he looked pleased with his act of revenge.

'I'll never forget the look on Denis's face,' Martin Buchan told me. 'I thought you were supposed to look happy when you scored a goal.' He looked as though he had just seen a ghost rather than popped one into the onion bag. And in a sense he had: a ghost of all those glories he had shared in, a memory of 236 goals in 393 appearances, a spectre of the good times. So distraught was he by sending his beloved reds down that it was his last kick in league football.

'Denis looked so shocked, but it wasn't Denis who sent us down,' recalled Morgan. 'We knew we were going down from Christmas, we just couldn't put the ball in the net. But when it finally happened, when he back-heeled that ball in, it was numb, it was an awful feeling. I'd never been in a relegated team in my whole career. It was something I wouldn't want again.'

The Morgan trophy cabinet? There were no plans to expand it just yet.

There certainly wasn't to be any silverware from the 1974 World Cup in Germany that summer, either, when Scotland, Morgan to the fore, did what they always do at major championships, and caught the first available plane back to Glasgow. During a slightly longer summer break than he had anticipated, Morgan was playing tennis and was hit by a ball in the eye. It detached a retina, an injury still visible to this day. In hospital, recovering from an operation, the invalid received a morale-boosting visit from Docherty who told him that, whatever happened, the new six-year contract he had negotiated for his captain would be honoured and that he would be getting a testimonial.

'He told me he had persuaded the board to make a special dispensation,' said Morgan. 'He told me how they decided not to grant any more testimonials, but they'd make an exception in my case. It wasn't true; there have been loads of testimonials since. But that's what he told me. And I believed him.'

But 1974–75 was not to be a happy season for Morgan. He was to discover what it was to be someone Tommy Docherty didn't want in his team. The hospital visits, the back slapping, the *bonhomie*, the endless promises of more money and better contracts, they stopped. Immediately. Docherty turned because he felt that the eye operation had taken its toll on his captain, that he had lost his timing. From October 1974 on, he began to blame any ills in the club on Morgan. He was constantly substituted even when playing well; in January 1975 he had the captaincy taken away from him and handed to Martin Buchan; in March 1975 Steve Coppell, a brilliant young winger from Tranmere, was brought in, demonstratively by the boss as a replacement for Morgan. Then there was the incident that was reported quickly back to Morgan. It concerned the Doc, deep in his cups, at a Catholic Sportsmen's dinner (there's a concept), swaying on the top table to his own version of the Morgan chant.

Willie, Willie Morgan, Willie Morgan on the wing,
He's a c**t, I'm gonna sort him out,
He'll be on his way out,
Before the end of the season.

Morgan, you will appreciate, quickly sensed something was up.

What he didn't realise was the lengths to which Docherty was going in his campaign to remove the last great Busbyite from the club. The board minutes from October 1974 indicate that the manager several times informed the directors that Morgan had sought a transfer and that he recommended the request should be turned down. Morgan claims he never made any such request.

'Why should I?' he said, 21 years on, but the taste still nasty in his mouth. 'I had a six-year contract, a testimonial promised; I wanted to fight for my place. I wanted to stay a United player.'

That goal, then, in November 1974, that Jon and I attempted to re-enact in the park weekly, or rather weakly, thereafter, meant a lot to Morgan. His look, that we had taken as one of simple, unblemished cool, was in fact directed at his tormentor-in-chief on the bench. With it he was saying, hey, cop that, Doc, not bad for a one-eyed man, eh? 'Actually what I was saying,' Morgan told me, 'was "up yours".'

In May 1975, immediately after United had regained their place in the first division and Morgan had sat out the last 11 games as Coppell excelled, Docherty took the players on a tour of Iran, the Far East and Australia. All except Morgan. 'He came to me,' Morgan remembered of the Doc, 'and said: "Look, I want us to be friends; let's forget what's happened. What I'd like you to do is I don't want you to come on the tour. Take the wife and kids and the club will pay for a holiday and I'll see you when I get back." The next thing I see is the front page of *The Manchester Evening News*, "Morgan refuses to go on tour."'

It was the standard Docherty trick: alert the press, ever hungry for a quote from the boss, and let them ferment discontent. Morgan, furious, did precisely what the Doc wanted: he confronted him. He demanded a meeting and took along his solicitor for insurance. Docherty told him it would be in the best interests of the club if he left. Morgan refused to go. Docherty said to him, 'If you remain at this club you will not play in the first team, the second, the third or any other team.'

Morgan pointed out he was owed a testimonial; Docherty offered him an *ex-gratia* payment of £5,000, which his lawyer advised him to refuse. Morgan, a proud and stubborn man, asked, then, for a transfer. 'I didn't want to leave, for lots of reasons,' he said. 'But I had no option but to leave. He left me with no options.' That summer, he was sold by Docherty to Burnley for £30,000, about a quarter of his true worth.

That was the Docherty way. Throughout his football career, he seemed to need enemies to function, needing the creative tension of ill will. If no enemies were around, he would create them. Never mind that a football team is a delicate coalition of egos; he always fell to the temptation to stir: dropping hints to the press, bad-mouthing players to fans he met casually around town, being tricky as a matter of course. Lou Macari, for instance, recalls an occasion when Docherty called him into his office and told him, quite unexpectedly, that he was going to make him the highest-paid player in the club, on a basic far higher than anyone else. The Doc, who liked a drink, had to pop out to the loo and, while he was gone, Macari checked out one or two papers on his desk. The top one was a list of proposed salaries which read: 'Lou Macari £300 a week; Martin Buchan £350 a week.'

It is impossible to be objective about Tommy Docherty. Attitudes to him are forged by a schizophrenia at the heart of his dealings with people. When on the right side of him, players found him a wonderful, inspirational, caring parent: a shrewd judge like Steve Coppell, for example, cannot speak too highly of him. On the wrong side, however, and they were simply out. And his real problem was that it was the young players on the right side, the older on the wrong. In the end, simple chronology dictated that everyone he dealt with always would, eventually, end up on the wrong side. At United the list is a tidy line-up: Denis Law, Tony Dunne, Pat Crerand, Ted MacDougall, George Best, Jim McCalliog, Jim Holton, Gerry Daly, George Graham and Willie Morgan.

The Doc himself remembers the end of Willie Morgan's time at Old Trafford very differently from the player. 'He came to me all the time that season, wanting a transfer,' Docherty told me when I interviewed him for the *Family Tree* documentary. 'I was duty-bound to tell the board of his requests, but I also advised them to turn them down. But your biggest enemy as a manager is an old pro in the dressing-room, poisoning the young minds, spreading the gospel – the wrong gospel, I might add. The best thing is to get them on their bikes as quickly as possible. So when he came to see me that summer, and said he wanted a transfer, I put it to the board and said: "This time, if that's what he wants, all right let's get him on his bike." And we did.'

So Willie Morgan went to Burnley, and Doc's Red Army hit the first division in August 1976 without my sartorial role model. Morgan came to Old Trafford hoping for the game's highest honours, but his stay at the club coincided with its worst spell since the war. Seven years after Matt Busby met him in a Burnley hotel room, Morgan left with just one record to his name: he is the longest-serving Manchester United player never to win a top medal.

'Oh thanks, yeah, remind me,' he said, when I reminded him. 'Thing is, I had a great time until the end. I played with wonderful players, that team I joined – Stiles, Crerand, Law, Bestie, Bobby – you know, that was some team. I have absolutely no regrets.'

And there was one thing, Morgan thought, as he left Old Trafford for Turf Moor: at least he wouldn't come across Tommy Docherty again.

What we hope, we journalists, when we interview a footballer, is that they might say something more interesting than 'at the end of day' or 'all credit to the lads'. We want not so much dirt as gossip, those little snap-shots of our heroes' lives, crumbs that give us a sense that they are as full of the same insecurities and dislikes as the rest of us. Managers know this, that's why they stop players talking to us, why they encourage the FA to bring in disrepute charges, why at Manchester United these days they train the young players to spot the media's crafty, winkling ways and to respond with blandness. When Granada Television invited Willie Morgan, then running Bolton Wanderers' midfield, on to their weekly football magazine *Kick Off* one evening in June 1977, they got what they were hoping for.

Morgan was asked on to comment about the Tommy Docherty affair. Docherty at the time had just danced round Wembley wearing the lid of the FA Cup on his head, and, sensing he was now unassailable, had announced he was having an affair with the wife of the club physio Laurie Brown. 'Who's up Mary Brown,' fans would sing, to the tune of the old Cockney drinking song, whenever the Doc subsequently made an appearance at a football ground.

At first, the club chairman Louis Edwards and his son Martin found this no cause for concern and stood by their manager. But by June speculation was rising that Matt Busby could not tolerate such behaviour in the manager of Manchester United and was seeking the Doc's removal. So, the presenter Gerald Sindstadt wondered, what did Willie Morgan, Busby's great confidante, reckon? 'Tommy Docherty's about the worst manager there has ever been,' said Morgan, revelling in his moment of public revenge. 'Nearly all the

Manchester United supporters will be delighted when he goes. Only then will United be a good club again.'

Well, I for one United supporter, was baffled. Like most of the naïve young occupants of the Stretford End, I worshipped the Doc. He'd just won us the Cup, we'd been playing the best football since Busby, sure he was shagging the physio's wife, but didn't that just confirm him as the lad we all wanted him to be? The Doc's public image, constructed with the assistance of a dozen obeisant journos, gave us not a hint of the way he really operated or of the number of enemies he had made in five years at United. I remember sitting watching that programme and seeing Morgan and thinking: What are you on about? Has your hair gone to your brain?

Soon afterwards, Docherty's solicitor wrote to Granada asking for an apology and seeking substantial damages for 'the pain and distress caused by Morgan's remarks'. Granada responded with the standard go-boil-your-head reply to libel threats: Morgan was merely and clearly stating a matter of opinion, they said. No compensation will be forthcoming. Out of courtesy they told Morgan of the letter, but told him not to worry about it, as there was no case to answer. A month later Morgan received a writ for libel, seeking damages against him and Granada Television.

For a year, Willie Morgan compiled evidence to prove his contention that the Doc was about the worst manager there has ever been. Even if he lost the case, there was something cathartic about the exercise. Twenty-nine examples of Doc double-dealing he gathered, sworn affadavits of mismanagement and personal misconduct. Morgan still has the affadavits in the attic of his house, ready if needed. All the enemies Doc made on the way up at United joined the queue to give him a good kicking on the way down: Pat Crerand was prepared to give evidence about how he saw Doc taking money for a scam. King Denis was willing to break his five-year silence over the way in which he was removed from the club he had graced. Alex Stepney would give evidence about how the players' pool was diminished by the Doc's interventions. Even Barry Fry was in there, with a story of how Docherty had demanded £1,000 to allow George Best to play for Dunstable Town, whom Fry was managing at the time. Nevertheless, Morgan was frightened. If he lost the case he could lose his house, his livelihood and everything he had risked his shins for.

And the case, down at the High Court in the Strand, was, as it were, going to be a bit of a trial for him. It was expected to last a month, and, warned his solicitor, if half of what he claimed about Docherty was true, it was going to get bloody.

Of all the mistakes Tommy Docherty has made, he will tell you now that taking Willie Morgan to court was the biggest. His contention was that Morgan, in an off-hand remark in a local television sports chat show watched by fewer people than tune in regularly to the test card, had damaged his reputation as a 'fair-dealing, right-minded manager'. What damaged it beyond any patch-up job was the court case, reported with salivating relish on the front pages of every national newspaper. In the privilege of the court all sorts of things which could never be written were able to be said and thence repeated in the media.

Worse, for the Doc, a degree of consistency is required when delivering evidence under oath. For most people this is no onerous task: just speak the truth. For policemen, continuity of evidence is equally simply attained: concoct a version of events that suits your purpose before the trial and stick to it rigidly throughout. But the Doc had grown so used to giving different interpretations of the same incident to different people at different times that he had long since lost sight of what was the proper order of events. The case proved, he now admits, 'a disaster'.

From day one of the trial, Monday, 13 November 1978, it was clear Tommy Docherty was not going to make a great character witness for himself. He was the first one up there, hand on the bible, taking the oath. Young footballers he had no problem handling; grown men in gowns and wigs with big vocabularies and a chess player's eye for weakness were another issue. Up there in the dock, the scale of the High Court seemed to diminish Docherty. The bullish egotist shrank; in his place stood a jittery, subdued, deferential husk, 'yes, Sir, no Sir'-ing his way through his counsel's examination. A neutral observer would have felt sorry for him, standing there alone in the dock, against the weight of evidence: a man without a script. Willie Morgan didn't, though.

'When Docherty started to give his evidence, being cross-examined by his brief, my barrister told me to tug him on the gown when he told a lie,' remembered Morgan. 'I just sat there tugging his jacket continuously until in the end he told me to back off, I was ruining his tailoring.'

On Tuesday, 14 November 1978, the second day of the case, the Doc was asked by Peter Bowsher, his counsel, to tell the court how he had transferred Denis Law. Docherty's account was almost word for word the same one he gave me when I interviewed him 18 years after the case. 'I got him in,' the Doc said to me, his eyelids flickering with unnatural speed as he spoke. 'I got him early, I might add, to give him plenty of warning, and told him I was going to give him a free transfer, so that he had plenty of time to sort himself out.'

Not quite: what happened was that Law was told by Docherty that he was not going to be transferred, that he was to be granted a testimonial (that word again), that he was in the scheme of things for the following season. And then, when King Denis had gone to Aberdeen to visit his sick mother, he had seen on the television that he was to be transferred. As Doc spoke that day, Willie Morgan turned and looked at Pat Crerand. At that point he knew he'd won.

On the third day of the trial, Wednesday, 15 November 1978, Morgan arrived in court as usual in his dark suit and white shirt, hair spilling over the collar. He had still to give evidence: the lawyers were enjoying toying with the Doc too much to let him out early. That day it was defence counsel, Morgan's brief John Wilmers QC's, chance to get in on the fun, cross-examining Docherty. Almost the first subject Wilmers raised was Denis Law. At the mention of the name, Docherty's face, Morgan recalled, started to twitch. Wilmers put to Docherty a version of events somewhat at odds with the one he had already given. He suggested to Docherty that although he had told Law he wouldn't put him on the transfer list and would grant him a testimonial, in fact he told television and press men that Law was on the list and could go.

'That was an outrageous thing to do,' Wilmers said. 'It was a wrong thing to do. It was very wrong,' replied Docherty, looking at the wooden floor of the dock. 'No decent competent manager would dream of treating a man like Law in that way,' suggested Wilmers. 'It was a wrong thing for a manager to do,' said Docherty. 'Definitely.'

Wilmers then pointed out to Docherty that he had told another version of the Denis Law story, under oath, the previous day when being cross-examined by his own brief. 'You told a pack of lies about

32

this incident to the jury,' pressed Wilmers. There was a pause. 'Yes,' said Docherty, quietly. 'Yes, it turned out that way. Yes.' That evening Docherty withdrew his suit. Outside the High Court, Morgan and Crerand, the old Busbyites, were photographed celebrating, grinning at the final triumph. Although a chortling Crerand did express a little disappointment that he didn't get in the dock: he had a thing or two to say, he said.

Revenge, a dish best eaten cold.

Docherty was ordered to pay costs, estimated at £30,000. In 1981 he was tried for perjury committed during his evidence in the libel trial. The case was thrown out. It was decided that Docherty did not deliberately set out to mislead anyone, it was just that, every time he opened his mouth, a mistruth popped out. I asked Docherty what he thought of the court case now, all these years later, when he's comfortable and happy and still with Mary. And he said something very bizarre. He said: 'At least I can put my head on the pillow at night knowing I never did anyone any harm. They can't, Morgan, Crerand, Law. They can't.'

Excuse me?

'They tried to put me in prison. Those three. I wouldn't do that to my worst enemy; I wouldn't do it to Saddam Hussein.'

Morgan looked puzzled indeed when I repeated this to him. 'We tried to put him in prison?' he said, incredulous. 'But he took *me* to court.'

After he won the case, Willie Morgan stayed in his house. And in 1996, he's still there. What a life he has had, constantly paid for doing what he loves. First it was football. He was playing eight years after Docherty reckoned he hadn't the eyes for it any more, first for Bolton and Blackpool, clubs within easy reach of his house, and then, during the summer, milking the American circuit, playing in Minnesota and Chicago. He finally stopped playing in May 1982, after 30 games for Blackpool.

'I never retired, you know,' he said, smiling. 'I just didn't sign the contract they offered me. I've never retired. Football was good to me. If it hadn't been for that piece of leather, kicking it around, I'd have been down the pit with my dad. Thank God, or whatever, whoever's up there. Thank you.'

Always canny financially (while at Bolton he had invested in a chain of launderettes, which helped the cash flow no end), in 1981 he moved into the corporate hospitality business. He was in it at the beginning, through the yuppie boom, he was big enough to survive the recession, he was established enough to exploit the economic up-turn. His speciality is organising celebrity golf tournaments for big companies (Shell is a client) in which executives pay to have a round with celebs. And one of the celebs generally turns out to be, well, Willie Morgan.

Tommy Docherty, though, is never invited for a round. The rancour at being removed so capriciously from the stage he craved still cuts Morgan. He may have won the case, but he still hates the man. 'Tommy Docherty did one thing for me, though; something I have to be grateful for,' he said. I expected some gag to follow, some pithy put-down of his enemy. But no, he meant it. 'When we were in Rome, playing Lazio I think in a friendly, he came into the hotel and said he'd organised an audience with the Pope for the team and that this wasn't an option, this was an order: we were all going. Well, we moaned and groaned like we always did, saying we had an important game of cards to play, but he insisted. And, you know what? It was great, fantastic, one of the greatest days of my life. Being in that room with the Pope – fantastic. So, thanks Tom.'

When I asked Docherty if he remembered coercing the players into a Papal audience, he denied it. He said he hadn't. 'No,' he said. 'No, no. It was voluntary. Most of them took advantage of it, but it was voluntary. No, no, of course I didn't make them go see him. There's no way I'd make my players do something they didn't want to.'

THE MAN WHO MADE MOTTY

Martin Buchan. Life began: 4.3.72

We have much to be grateful to Martin Buchan for: his calmness, his precision tackling in times of crisis, his presence at the back for 11 years at Manchester United. But it must be recorded that he is, at least partially, responsible for another, less palatable, aspect of football: if it wasn't for Martin Buchan the career of John Motson might never have taken off. In 1977 David Coleman, the BBC's regular Cup final commentator, was in contractual dispute with the corporation, and a young Motty was promoted from third string on *Match of the Day* to cover the big one.

'I'd done some research before the game and I'd read that the number of steps up to the royal box was 39,' Motty told me when I interviewed him before the 1992 final. 'Nothing in that until I remembered the name of the Manchester United captain, and then a little phrase came to me, so I wrote it down. I hadn't been satisfied at all by my performance during the game and I think that a number of people who had been watching me were thinking rather the same. They were rather impressed, though, when that ad lib came out at the end. But of course it wasn't an ad lib; I'd written it down. I promise you, though, it's the only time it's happened, that I've written something down.'

And the little phrase in question, the fake ad lib that saved Motty's bacon and set him on course for a career telling us that – ho-ho – would you believe it, the linesman on the far side is only one of four left-handed linesmen on the Premiership list? It was: 'How appropriate that a man named Buchan should climb the 39 steps to the royal box to lift the Cup.'

35

Thus the first question to ask of Martin Buchan is this: what does he think of the great phrase that launched a million Motticisms? Is he proud? Ecstatic? Guilty? 'I'm aware of it,' he said, playing with the deadest of bats, when I asked him. 'As it happens, I might not have played in that game. We'd played at West Ham on the Monday night before the final, got a 4–1 hiding and I opened up my knee ligaments after that athletic specimen Trevor Brooking fell over my leg. We were staying down in London for the week and I said to Tommy Doc: "You might as well give me the train ticket and send me back home, I'll not be fit for Saturday." I didn't train all week, then on the morning of the final the Doc said to me: "What do you think?" And I said: "I'll give it a go." After about five minutes I had a little tussle in the centre circle with Tommy Smith and my knee held out. I thought, if it can survive him, I'll be all right. And I was.'

Which was just as well for John Motson. 'How appropriate that a man named Stepney should climb the 39 steps to the royal box to lift the Cup' doesn't have quite the same literary ring to it at all.

Between 1956 and 1994, the careers of three players overlapped and span across Manchester United history: Bobby Charlton (1956–73), Martin Buchan (1972–83) and Bryan Robson (1981–94). For dedication to the cause they have few equals. Yet for Martin Buchan at least, things might have been very different. But for an unfortunate injury to a predecessor, the shrewd-eyed Scot might have gone elsewhere. When, towards the end of the 1972 season, Aberdeen decided that their young captain could try his luck south of the border, to let him, as he says, 'see if the English game was as good as the English said it was,' the rush to sign Martin Buchan turned into a stampede. Leeds wanted him, Liverpool were very keen, but it was Manchester United he chose. An odd decision, it might be thought, since Liverpool and Leeds were in the ascendant at the time and United were in the latter stages of a precipitous decline. But there was, as it would become clear there usually was with Buchan, method at work here.

'I looked at Leeds and I saw a guy called Norman Hunter,' he explained when I asked him the question he must have asked himself pretty shortly after signing: Why? 'I looked at Liverpool and I saw a guy called Tommy Smith. I looked at United and I saw David Sadler was struggling with an injury and they needed a replacement. It was the fact United could offer me first-team football that swung it. People have said to me, if you'd joined Liverpool or Leeds you'd have won so much more. Maybe. But who's to say I'd have ever made the first team?'

Signing Buchan in 1972 for £125,000 was the one thing manager Frank O'Farrell did of lasting significance at Manchester United. But typically of the pecking-order behind the scenes at Old Trafford back then, it was not O'Farrell Buchan remembers from the day he signed.

'We met up in Belshill,' he said in the careful, measured speaking manner he has. 'Which, as you may recall, was Matt Busby's birthplace. Sir Matt was up there to visit his mother who was ill at the time. So it seemed convenient for all of us to meet up there. It was 29 February 1972. I went with Aberdeen's manager. I was flattered that United had brought out the big guns, the heavy artillery you might say, to meet me. Sir Matt and Les Olive [the club secretary] were there. And Frank O'Farrell, obviously.'

Buchan was exactly what United needed: a class centre-back. Although only 5ft 10ins he made up what he lacked in height with pace, vision and a Maldini-like ability to read what was on opposing forwards' minds. He lifted the Scottish Cup as Aberdeen captain at 21 and very few of his contemporaries were surprised that he was snapped up in England. 'I think if O'Farrell had signed Buchan at the beginning of that season instead of the end,' Alex Stepney reckons, 'we might have won something that year and Frank might have been saved. He would have made that much difference.'

Getting into the first team at Old Trafford was no problem for a man of Buchan's class, and he made his debut almost immediately the paperwork was completed, against Spurs at White Hart Lane on 4 March 1972. The team that day was: Stepney, O'Neil, Dunne, Buchan, James, Sadler, Morgan, Gowling, Charlton, Law, Best; the score was 2–0 to Spurs; the crowd was 54,814.

Indeed Buchan was somewhat shocked by how easy it was for the newcomer to break into the team. 'It was a strange mix,' he said, when I interviewed him during a break in Euro 96, when he was working flat-out in his job supplying Puma kit and boots to participating teams. 'There were world-class players coming to the end of their careers either through time – like Bobby and Denis – or choice – like George – playing alongside players I did not feel were good enough to get into Aberdeen's reserve team. Now that might seem a harsh thing to say. But we played Aberdeen in a friendly as part of my deal and we lost up there 5–2 so maybe I wasn't too far from the truth.'

Wasn't he alarmed about it? 'Losing 5–2 at Aberdeen?' No, the standard of the team he found. 'Well, it wasn't quite what I'd hoped for.'

Buchan did not come from the standard Scottish footballing background, the industrial south-west. And for him football was not the escape route from poverty it was for many. It was not a choice for Martin Buchan of foundry or football; he had done well at school, he had qualifications. He would, if he had not been so good at the game, have become a teacher (like his brother George, who played a couple of games for United as a substitute, making the pair, for a game or two, the precursor of the Greenhoffs and the Nevilles). Buchan shared few of the enthusiasms of the average footballer either. He had no fondness for the turf, he preferred a good book to the card school, he was meticulously dressed in an old-fashioned sort of way – what your mum would call smart. As they say in football circles of those out-of-step with the laddy norm: he kept himself to himself. Moreover, the quiet, reserved, distant newcomer found few of his noisier colleagues anxious to integrate him into the dressing-room.

'Buchan just wasn't one of the lads,' remembers Willie Morgan, who most definitely was. 'He was different. The first time I heard him speak was about a month after he joined. After training one day George was looking for some change to make a phone call, and no one had any money, we were all in track suits and so on. And then suddenly Buchan pipes up: "Here you are, George, here's 2p." And we all thought: "He talks after all." But we thought no more about it until about two weeks later, when we were going to an away game, and he comes down the back of the bus and says to George: "Any chance of having that money back I lent you?" And George hasn't a clue: "What money?" And Buchan goes: "The money for the phone call I lent you."'

Worse than simply being perceived as different, unbeknown to him Buchan was cast by others in the great internecine feud that was enveloping the club. He was seen as Frank's boy, the one who always sat at the front of the team bus away from the lads, creeping up to the boss. It was a role that was ascribed to him the moment, in only his second game, he was made captain in place of the injured Bobby Charlton. That decision, the rest of the side felt, made it clear what O'Farrell thought of them.

'At the time I didn't realise what was going on,' Buchan told me. 'But I suppose with the benefit of hindsight there was a fair bit of scheming around. Nobody told me about it, because I was seen to be on the other side. I don't think Best was involved and I know Bobby wasn't. Bobby at that time seemed much more concerned about his own position, coming to the end of his career. That's not to be derogatory, we all reach our sell-by date, but Bobby seemed very withdrawn. It was others. There were others more interested in destroying Frank than in the good of the club.'

And who were these plotters? 'They know who they are,' he said, giving as little away as he did when marshalling United's back line. 'Under Sir Matt, they had grown up with a philosophy of go out and enjoy yourselves. That's all very well, but you can only enjoy yourself if you are doing the job right. I think a lot of them resented the efforts of Frank and Malcolm [Musgrave, O'Farrell's coach] to bring a bit more organisation to the team. The trouble was at the time, all the other teams were getting organised.'

In a way, his team-mates were right: Martin Buchan was in another faction. But over time it would emerge it wasn't the one they assumed. It was a faction of one: the Martin Buchan faction. 'I had a reputation for being a bit of a loner, but that's because I didn't like cards,' Buchan recalled. 'And later I had a reputation for being stubborn, but that's because I wasn't prepared to do things which I thought were unnecessary.'

It soon became clear what those things were. Things like refusing to hand in his passport to the club for safe keeping ('I was an adult, I felt I was capable of remembering my own passport when we went abroad'). Or things like, on the day during a foreign tour when the team were told they could wear casual clothes to a function, turning up in blazer and tie and getting mistaken for the club chairman by the locals ('I'd brought along a blazer and tie assuming we would need smart wear and I thought, well I brought it, I might as well wear it. I wasn't being difficult. Heaven forbid'). Or things like his attitude to the press (a journalist once approached Buchan in the car park of the Cliff – United's training ground – and asked if he could have a quick word. 'Aye,' came the speedy reply as Buchan walked swiftly to his car, 'velocity').

As Willie Morgan said: different.

Whatever was going on, six months after Martin Buchan arrived, the man who signed him was sacked. A dispiriting and rather alarming event, presumably, to see your mentor, one of the few people at the club willing to exchange words with you, evicted so soon after you arrived. 'Not really,' Buchan told me. 'Players are funny, they might say they're disappointed when a manager is sacked, and maybe they are disappointed. But there's always another one comes along.'

And the other one, in this instance, was Tommy Docherty. The Doc was the man who had given Buchan his first Scottish cap and presumably liked what he saw. 'Not really,' Buchan recalled. 'The Doc made it difficult for me at first. I think he thought I was too short to play in the middle, so he played me at left-back. I wasn't happy and at one time it looked like I might leave the club. Doc came up to me one day and said Dave Sexton, funnily enough, had put in a £160,000 bid for me and would I be prepared to go to QPR. I thought I'd call his bluff, so I said yes. Nothing came of it and I was soon playing centre-back. I think at the time Doc was listening to one or two of the voices who had got him appointed . . . '

And who might they be?

'They know who they are. Anyway, I won the Doc over.'

Indeed he did. In the year United went down, with Buchan organising the defence from his favoured position, they leaked fewer goals than in any year since they won the title in 1967. Docherty realised that his back line was in safe hands for another ten years, all he needed now was a goal-scorer and he would have a team. But wasn't the ambitious young Buchan, who had been courted by the two teams then at the top of the league, at that point not keen to find an employer with whom he might win things? Not much point coming down from Scotland to see what English football was all about and discovering it was all about the second division.

'I wasn't happy about relegation,' he said. 'No one at the club was. But I decided to stay to try and help the club back into the first division. After all, I was one of the players involved in getting them into the second division; I felt I had a certain responsibility for getting them back up.'

And how easy it turned out to be, tearing away with the second division championship with a style and purpose wholly lacking during the bleak relegation years, hammering Cardiff, Orient and Fulham. Not just on the pitch, but on the terraces too, United made their presence felt in Division Two. Every away game, Doc's Red Army were making their mark on market towns across the country, demolishing ageing, inadequate stadia with the enthusiasm of Lord Justice Taylor and all the time establishing their reputation as the biggest hooligans in Britain.

'I remember the game we clinched promotion at Notts County there were all sorts of battles going on on the terraces,' Buchan recalled. 'It got so bad you could hardly concentrate on your game, and you thought: "Do we really need this?" But for the most part that season I wasn't aware of trouble. I wonder, maybe I was so wrapped up in my own little world, I just didn't notice.'

But the image I remember most from the second division adventure was the day I went to Old Trafford to watch United beat Blackpool 4–0 and saw the team jog the diminutive and lack-lustre championship trophy around the touchline, dozens of small boys in bad tank-tops in their wash. Buchan was in there, resplendent that day in an Adidas track suit top he had slipped on, while everyone else seemed happy to remain in their Umbro team shirts. The one-man faction in action again.

'The team had just signed a boot deal with a manufacturer whose product I considered inferior. Boots are the tools of your trade, they have to be right,' he told me, 21 years on, by way of explanation for an act which, if repeated these days by the skipper of Manchester United, would cause such marketing repercussions that millions would be wiped off the stock market value of several companies. 'I stuck with my own boots, and if I wasn't going to wear the new boots, naturally I wasn't going to wear that company's track suit. I don't think I was being difficult.'

But whatever he was wearing, Buchan could not disguise his facial cast. It was not the face of Stuart Pearce after scoring that Euro 96 penalty he was wearing that day. There was no hint of triumph; his expression, as I recall, was rather one of embarrassment. He and Lou Macari in particular looked thoroughly shamefaced.

'The second division was never as easy as Macari now says it was,' said Buchan. 'He might have had an easy time up front, but as a defender you still have forwards to mark. And one good thing, it allowed us to get used to winning, which is rather nice and was important the next year. But yes, you're right, it was embarrassing to collect second division medals. We felt we and the club should never have been in that position.'

Buchan accrued more than a winner's medal to his name that year. The season of rebuilding downstairs coincided with Buchan receiving the captaincy, which the Doc presented to him in January 1975. After it had been stripped from Willie Morgan.

'It was ironic, Willie and the Doc,' Buchan told me, in a tone which suggested the irony rather amused him. 'When Doc first came to the club, the expression I'd use, if I wasn't so careful, is: "They were as thick as thieves." And then they fell out. Doc was so silly to sue him for libel. I mean, there was only one thing he needed to say after Willie had said that on the television: "Sour grapes." And we'd have all known what he meant.'

And when he said that, I thought: It's going to be fun having him and Morgan in the same dream dressing-room.

As United stormed back into the first division, Buchan finally, after three and half years at the club, was where he wanted to be: challenging for the top honours. 'They were the happiest days of my career,' he said. 'Those two years under Doc back in the first division, we felt we could give any side two goals start at Old Trafford and still beat them, that was the feeling in the club.'

And Buchan was much happier with other elements of his working life than at any time since he arrived. In one of the great chalk-and-cheese pairings in sport, he had been partnered, for away-match-room-sharing purposes, with Lou Macari. What a double-act: the idiosyncratic loner with the chummy, self-appointed piss-taker in chief. It was like rooming John McEnroe with Bjorn Borg, Ian Botham with Mike Brearley, Gazza with Alan Shearer. It worked from the off.

'Lou and I roomed together and stripped next to each other in the dressing-room for ten years,' Buchan said. 'We were the odd couple when you think about it. He liked horses, I couldn't stand gambling. He never had a drink in his life, I liked a pint. Yet football-wise we were very much on the same wavelength.'

Macari himself remembers he only got the job of rooming with the skipper because someone had to. 'A lot of people misunderstood

Martin,' Macari told me when I interviewed him for the United Family Tree programme. 'Because he was very smart, very meticulous, very thorough in his preparation, people got the wrong idea. Because he had his ways, his routines, people steered clear of him. I didn't. True, he wasn't one for watching television all night in the room, and he liked everything to be very tidy. But once you got to know him, once you understood his sense of humour, you realised what a man he was.'

Though they may have been room-mates, the shy, different Aberdonian was never tempted to become Macari's partner-in-gaggery. 'No, no,' Buchan said. 'Ashley Grimes was his apprentice. They particularly enjoyed themselves at airports, I remember. They'd see someone coming in the opposite direction laden down with bags and one of them would stand behind the victim while the other would walk up to them, with their hand outstretched, going "Hi, how you doing", and the man would have to put his bag down, to shake hands. And then they'd walk straight past him and shake hands with each other. Or they used to dangle a pound note on a piece of string from off the balcony and when someone stooped to pick it up, they'd pull it away.'

So if he wasn't a perpetrator, was he ever a victim of such pranks? 'Me?' said Buchan, incredulous at the thought he might be so silly. 'No. I never bend over to pick up less than a tenner.'

It was Buchan's contention that the Doc's new team, infused with spirit, passion and skill, could have won the championship in 1976, and made it nine rather than 26 years between titles. But at the last, even though they led the table in March, their young eyes were taken from the prize by the thought, as they stormed to the FA Cup final, of Wembley. 'We could have won the league,' he said. 'We were used to winning, we started off well, it was the best chance of winning it I had in my career. But I feel a few of my colleagues were seduced by the glamour of the Cup.'

And in the event, even that was snatched away from them by a tenacious and experienced Southampton side. After that game, Buchan was furious, incandescent at some of his team-mates' attitudes. 'I think it would be a lot better if players' pools were banned and they let the players concentrate on the job in hand,' he told me. 'It's amazing how many of our players saw pound signs in their eyes the first time the mere mention of the word Wembley arose. In the end, players made very little out of it after they'd paid tax. Much ado about nothing.'

But why would money interfere with performance?

'On the day too many of our players were too distracted by the peripheries. Too many of them thought all we had to do was turn up and we'd go home with medals. They were right, we did. Losers' medals.'

And the guilty men that grim May day, who were they?

'They know who they are.'

A few evenings after that Cup final flop, at a banquet held at the Midland Hotel, Manchester, which was planned as a victory parade and turned out to be a collective drowning of sorrows, Martin Buchan's stalwart defence of the one faction at United he always steadfastly supported, the Martin Buchan faction, was again widely misinterpreted. He was called upon to say the captain's customary few words of thanks after the dinner was finished. But he refused. When the time came, he walked to the top table, had a word in Les Olive's ear and, much to the embarrassment of the assembled company, immediately sat down again. In an outfit as political as United was back then, Buchan's action was bound to be interpreted by club Kremlinologists as an act of significance. Some felt he was angry about the bad performance, others decided it was part of contractual manoeuvres, still others saw it as a late conversion to the anti-Docherty cause (one prominent sack-the-Doc activist swears to this day Buchan told him before the dinner that he would not speak on the same platform as 'that man').

Characteristically, however, Buchan's reasons turned out to be solely to do with the Martin Buchan faction. 'I arrived at the banquet and saw on the menu that I was supposed to be making a speech,' he recalled. 'Well, that was the first I'd heard of it. No one had told me. I felt if I was going to have to stand up and say something in front of all those people I ought to have been given the chance to prepare. So when it was my turn, I simply refused to do it.'

In 1977, circumstances were considerably happier. Thanks to Jimmy Greenhoff's chest, United won the Cup and Buchan gave an after-dinner address. Tommy Docherty had promised as much, on the balcony of the town hall in Albert Square the year before, when hundreds of thousands of us – we are English after all – turned up to congratulate the losers. 'We'll be back next year, and we'll win it,' he'd said. For once he was as good as his word.

The skipper was at his best that day: smooth, controlled, elegant, blocking out Kevin Keegan in the permy one's last domestic game for Liverpool, ensuring the Scousers were restricted to a mere double: the league championship, and a few days later the European Cup. That afternoon, on the Wembley terraces, we reds exorcised the memories of the previous year and chanted, with all the magnanimity victory affords: 'Liverpool, Liverpool.'

Buchan was, at the end of an emotional afternoon, faced with the climb every footballer in England aspires to, the climb that drove John Motson into poetic orbit. 'I climbed the steps and there was this nice royal lady with the trophy,' Buchan said. 'But at the time I didn't want to waste time talking to her. I just wanted to get my hands on that trophy and show it to the fans. I turned my back on her almost as soon as she had said anything. She must have thought me very rude.'

And has he got a video of the game, then, a permanent memory of the moment Motty immortalised him?

'No,' he said, sharply. 'Well, I might have somewhere. But it's probably of ITV. I mean, what kind of a guy's going to count the number of steps up to the royal box. I mean, I ask you?'

Two years later, Buchan had a third appointment with the royal box. This time there was no Tommy Docherty; by then the Doc had been consumed by his own appetites. 'If anyone tells you they knew what was going on with the Doc, they're liars,' said Buchan, whose relationship with the manager was very different from Willie Morgan's. 'No one did; we were all amazed. Losing the Doc was a big disappointment; you never know what might have happened if he'd stayed. We had a very good side, with pace, a fair bit of experience and a lot of enthusiasm.'

Did the sacking affect the players, then?

'Some,' he said. 'But only weak players use the decisions of the board as an excuse. The strong get on with it.'

Instead, as the Cup final teams walked out that day at Wembley in 1979, Buchan was led out on to the turf by Dave Sexton, at the time in possession of the title presently held by Ray Wilkins: the nicest man in football.

'I'll tell you what kind of a guy Dave was,' Buchan said. 'The night before the '79 final, he presented us each with a watch he had bought out of his own pocket. There's not many a manager would have done that. And if you're reading this, Dave, mine needs a new battery.' Sexton felt that Docherty's team was too lightweight, too flibbertigibbet, and he strengthened the spine by acquiring Joe Jordan and Gordon McQueen from Leeds. Buchan, though, remained in residence at the back, sweeping up alongside the giant and sometimes impetuous McQueen. This formation had seen United to the final, trouncing Liverpool in a majestic performance in the semi.

I went to the final with my then girlfriend who lived two doors down from Buchan. We used to spend hours watching his house, checking for evidence of wild parties and late-night beer sessions with the lads. There was none. As the neighbours of men who defraud banks for millions say on *News At Ten*: he kept himself very much to himself. Nevertheless, she'd used her considerable charms and managed to winkle a ticket out of him. I'd got mine from a fellow student, who turned out to be the son of a Middlesbrough director and – perhaps this is no coincidence – no football fan. For most of the game I sat, a block away from her, in misery. After 80 minutes it was 2–0 to the Arsenal – no mean side with Brady, Stapleton, O'Leary, Rix. United were awful. Then McQueen scored; then, with two minutes to go, dancing through their defence, so did McIlroy. As the equaliser hit the net, I found myself in an embrace with a fat man who had been sitting next to me, stumbling and tumbling down the terraces in an ecstatic masque, bawling in each other's faces, a piece of male bonding as instant as anything in a San Franciso bath house. A minute later, Sunderland scored for them, and the two of us, our marriage plans put on hold, lay where we had fallen as a spotty Arsenal youth stood over us, shouting 'Why don't you two just fuck off back up North.' I think it was Nick Hornby.

My afternoon was completed on the tube back into central London, when a fellow United fan took one look at the badge I was wearing, read it slowly out loud – 'MUFC: Reds Against Racism' – and punched me in the face, because, he said, he may have been United, but he was NF.

Looking back on that goal in the highlights that evening, one thing struck me as I watched as Brady ran at United, as Macari and Thomas fell over themselves to let him through, as Brady passed to Rix, as Rix curled it over Bailey's girlie grasp, as Sunderland popped it in at the far post, as Sunderland ran off in a delirium, big blue collars flapping round his Paul Calf moustache, as Stapleton hung on to him, a stowaway on his shirt. What I thought was: where the hell was Martin Buchan? Where the hell was our Mr Reliable? Where the hell was the man you could trust when you needed him most?

'I tell you one of the reasons we lost that day,' he said, when I asked the question I had waited 17 years to ask. 'We lost because I played possibly the worst game I played in my entire Manchester United career that day. I was awful. And I don't think the goalkeeper had a very good game either.'

That game was axiomatic of United's team of the period: under Tommy Docherty they were greater than the sum of their parts; under Dave Sexton they were less. After nearly winning the Cup in 1979, after nearly winning the league in 1980, in 1981 the nearly man was to discover that at Old Trafford nearly is not close enough. For the third time in his United career, Martin Buchan saw his manager shown the door: Dave Sexton was sent to Coventry.

'Dave was a lovely man, but maybe the pressure at Old Trafford was too much for him,' Buchan reckoned. 'It was the press that did it. With Doc, they'd go round on a Friday afternoon, he'd take them up to his office, open a couple of bottles of wine and hold court. The problem they had with Doc was what to leave out, he did their job for them. Dave was never like that, he was very uneasy with them, he didn't give them anything. And the press didn't like Dave.'

He was right. They called him Whispering Dave in the Manchester press corps and had little competitions after press conferences to see who could best mimic his nervous habit of swallowing hard before he said anything.

The arrival of his fourth manager, Ron Atkinson, was to signal an upturn in the press corps' relations with Old Trafford. It was also to signal the end of Buchan's time at the club. Although he played 26 games in Big Ron's first year – as many as Kevin Moran and Gordon McQueen – it was made clear to him he had no future.

'Ron, er, well,' Buchan said, sighing at the memory. 'I have nothing against him, I think we just met at the wrong time. He came to the club and he looked at the birth certificates and he thought, oh aye 6.3.49, I'm not going to build a team around him. I was coming to the end of my career, he was looking to make a name for himself, it was inevitable. But I felt he wrote me off before my time. When he made it clear I wasn't going to be in the first team, I decided to go. That's the way it should be, I didn't want anyone thinking I was looking for a holiday. If I was upset at the time, it wasn't with him or the way he did it, it was because I wanted to stay.'

But Buchan did not leave before putting the manager firmly in his place in the manner in which he is a master. When the team played in Zaragosa, they were standing on the pitch and Ron came over to a group which included Bryan Robson and Buchan. 'Have you played here before?' he asked Buchan. 'Yes,' came the reply. 'I played here in an international match in 1969 when you were playing in the fourth division.'

Thus chronology catches up with even the most consistent. And the best centre-back United ever had this side of Steve Bruce was on his way out of the game, via a short stay at Oldham and an even shorter one as manager of Burnley for four months.

'I realised my love affair with the game finished when I finished playing,' he said. 'I had to become a manager to discover that. I found at Burnley I couldn't play Trivial Pursuit. I was very naïve, I thought everyone would be pulling in the same direction at a football club, but I had to spend all my time working out whose interests everyone was working in. The chairman, the players, they seemed to want different things from me. So I got out.'

At Burnley, it seemed, there were just far too many factions.

THE GORDON HILL JOKE
CONTINUES

Gordon Hill. Life began: 15.11.75

At the Cliff, Manchester United's training ground, most mornings you will find dozens of fans in track coats and replica nylon, just hanging around, imbibing the atmosphere. Souvenir-burdened families sit on a grassy bank and squint at training being conducted well out of ear-shot. Fathers point out Becksy, Eric and Peter Schmeichel for six-year-olds who seem far less interested than their dads. Mums fuss and cluck, making sure their offspring have got everything they want to be signed ready, just in case Giggsy is in a hurry. As training finishes and the players emerge, shining, from the showers, to drive off in their slick motors to important afternoon engagements with snooker halls or photographers' studios, a crowd folds around them, seeking signatures on posters, books, tea-cosies, or anything with the words Manchester and United in conjunction on them.

Most Fridays, as the players leave, you can spot a small, busy man arriving at the ground to take part in the weekly kickaround organised by Alex Ferguson for the non-playing staff. He has a fine plume of brown hair which bounces as he bob-walks on the balls of his feet, heels up. His eyes dart around, checking to see if he has been recognised, but the families, the schoolkids, don't seem to know. On his way in, he might pass a player on the way out, and he will chummily greet them in a shrill cockney: 'Awight Nicky?' 'Scholesy, yeah? Good on yer, son.' And the players look back, not knowing either, their eyes betraying what they're thinking: 'Who's that joker, then?'

But anyone with a long memory, who can mentally strip away a few pounds from the little man's jowls and smooth out a few wrinkles around the eyes, will know. They'll remember a left foot that could volley, they'll remember a presence on the edge of the penalty area at corners, lurking, ready to feed on lay-offs, gorge on bad clearances. They'll remember Hillsborough, 3 April 1976, when this little man and his left foot took United to the FA Cup final, blitzing two furious goals past a stricken Derby County. They'll remember Gordon Hill.

Of all the names that have made a difference at Manchester United in recent history, Hill's is the one most frequently forgotten. He doesn't appear in the television studios analysing matches, he's not a summariser for local radio, he's rarely the guest speaker at sportsmen's dinners. He's not in management, he hasn't made a fortune out of dry cleaning, he doesn't even own a pub. He makes a living coaching groups of small children near his home in Macclesfield and is trying to start a corporate hospitality sideline. But at the moment most Fridays he is free to pop down to the Cliff for the afternoon kickabout, in which Stuart Pearson, Martin Buchan, Arthur Albiston, Jimmy Ryan and other assorted lags discover that Alex Ferguson is as competitive in friendly games of seven-a-side as he is about the Premiership. Gordon Hill loves popping back, loves the banter of those games. It gives him a chance to relive those moments, the moments that burn brightest in his mind, when he was in the centre of things at United, when his mere appearance in the Cliff car-park would have initiated an autograph frenzy. When he meant something.

'I'm desperate,' he told me when I spoke to him one evening a couple of months after Becksy, Scholesy and the rest had won the double, when he'd just returned from a long session coaching schoolchildren. 'I'm desperate to be involved in the game. I used to be a pass master, now I'm a past master. I want to teach what I know. Sure I've got me kids, they exhaust me they do, the little rug rats. But I want to be back in the game, I'm wasted out here. I want a chance to pass on what I know to the next generation. You see, all I want is football. It's all I know. If I died on a football field, I'd be happy.'

According to those who know Gordon Hill, you either love him or you think he's a prat. For three years at Old Trafford there was no doubt which side you were on. Between 1975 and 1978 Gordon Hill's star burnt brighter than any. He epitomised an era. A glorious, short-lived, naïve period of spontaneous, beautiful football. An era, even when it was happening, you knew couldn't last, you knew would be suffocated by the advance of the coach, the march of Don Revie, the start of the Anfield beat. And what did Gordon Hill, the bobby-dazzler on the left wing, put it down to, that uninhibited time, that period of wonderful invincibility, those few months when the opposition felt defeated before the ref had even blown his whistle? Not courage. Not skill. Not preparation. He put it down to embrocation.

'Things weren't as plush at Old Trafford in them days,' he told me. 'Even the smell, it was not like your Imperial Leather, it was rough, like your linament. Blimey, it stank. We had this five oils stuff, a rubbing oil Laurie [Brown] used to put on us; he had it specially made. And what a stench. But it was like a warning stench. It permeated everything, through the skips and everything. It would linger. And when we went somewhere, taking all the kit with us, the smell came as well. People knew we were coming. They'd know who they were playing and they'd be frightened. They could smell us. And once they smelt us, they were gone.'

It began, Gordon Hill's Manchester United sniffing safari, with an insult from the club chairman: Louis Edwards called him a flash London bastard. Hard but fair.

'I remember exactly how it happened, how I came to be at United,' he recalls, the speed of delivery much as it was back then, back when he was at the centre of things. 'Millwall were due to play Yeovil in the Cup on that sloping pitch of theirs and so we were training on a pitch with a slope on it. At half-time they called me over and told me that the bank had told them they had to sell me. Otherwise they were going to – wossname, you know, oh blimey – foreclose, that's it. They pulled me off there and then cos they didn't want me to get injured. I didn't know where I was going till the next morning when I was told to be at Euston and I met the manager there and he told me I was on the train to Manchester. And I says: "What, City?" And he says: "No, United." I couldn't believe it: me going to Manchester United? Come on. Me playing in the same position as George Best? You're having a laugh. I arrived at Old Trafford and went through them big double doors they had in them days, up the marble staircase, and into this big office and there was Louis Edwards and TD himself. And Louis says to me after a couple of minutes: "You're a flash London bastard, we'll cut you down to size." It didn't put me off – nothing would have done – and I signed up there and then.

'That night I went to see United in the League Cup against City and they got stuffed 4–0, and I thought: "Oh my Gawd, this can't be true." The next morning I went down on the train back to London and I met up with the Millwall boys on the same train; they'd been playing Bury, I think. I was booked first class, but I was having none of that, so I went back with the boys and I said: "Here, guess what's happened to me."' And you can imagine, the Millwall lads must have been thrilled to see him back among them.

Hill, or, to give him his full title, Hilly, or Hills ('footballers have this habit of shortening yer name into a nickname, so they'd call me Hilly, or Hills, cos it was shorter; well it wasn't shorter, it was longer, but if you had a short name, they'd lengthen it'), cost £70,000, which, it turned out, was a snip, a steal, a piece of larceny on a grand scale. When he made his debut against Aston Villa on 15 November 1975 the team was: Stepney, Nicholl, Houston, Daly, B Greenhoff, Buchan, Coppell, McIlroy, Pearson, Macari, Hill; the score was 2–0; the scorers Coppell and McIlroy; the crowd 51,562. Never mind that he fell out with Willie and the rest; in 1976, Tommy Docherty could do no footballing wrong. Gordon Hill was the final piece in a glorious jigsaw.

Legend has it that when United looked relegation certainties from the early spring of 1974, Matt Busby said to Docherty: 'Let's go down in style.' If they didn't quite manage that, they certainly came back up in style, crushing all-comers in the second division. Yet that wasn't enough for the Doc. At the beginning of the 1975–76 season, he was still playing the 4–3–3 formation as established by Alf Ramsey in 1966 which became the standard in the '70s. The rotund Tommy Jackson had been brought in from Nottingham Forest and was trundling around the midfield to no great effect, but Docherty harboured a yen to return to wingers. Hill, paired with Steve Coppell on the right, would, he believed, make a devastating, attacking team. It was an unconventional view: Hill was not one to tackle back, he had a pathological aversion to playing in his own half, and besides, anyone who had read Eamonn Dunphy's *All in a Game*, an account of life at Millwall, wouldn't have taken the geezer on if they'd been paid.

'You never knew what he was going to do,' wrote Dunphy. 'Which makes him impossible to play with. And he gives away the ball too much. He has learnt a little, but I doubt his capacity to learn much. And he's not very good at picking people up. When you say to him: "Watch the full-back," he just watches him race away. He literally just watches him.'

More than that, Dunphy, you couldn't help feeling, fell firmly into the 'what a prat' camp when it came to opinion of young Gordon. Every other chapter in the book begins with 'The Gordon Hill joke continues' or 'We pulled a beauty on Gordon Hill today' or 'the Gordon Hill thing is still going on'.

Docherty, though, was partial to a gamble and, besides, he didn't read books. Hill was popped into the team and immediately sparkled. He had quick instincts, quick feet and an ability to scorch past full-backs, skills which gave him one of the best scoring records ever achieved by a winger at Old Trafford: 51 goals in 132 appearances (Coppell bagged 70 in 392, Kanchelskis 36 in 129, Morgan 33 in 291). And what we in the Stretford Paddock loved most was the number of those goals that were corkers. No tap-in merchant was Hilly: a bending rasper from outside the box against QPR, a zinger of a volley from a corner against Peterborough in the FA Cup, a blinder against City. It got to the point where you thought every corner United got he was going to score. He looked like a little bird of prey over a motorway verge, hovering 20 yards out, waiting.

'I used to watch *Match of the Day* of a Saturday,' he told me, 'and if there was a spectacular goal, a goal of the month or whatever, I'd say to myself, "Right, Hilly, you're gonna do better than that." And I'd go out on the Saturday consciously trying to do better than them. And a lot of the time I would – I'd do it. People say I was a great volleyer, that I was classed as one of the best in the world. But for me, at that time, I was *the* best. I'd train very hard, practising all the time, till it came to the point where I didn't want the ball on the deck, I wanted it to hang in the air. That meant I could try things others wouldn't. I felt I couldn't miss in them days. The years I was there, there was this sense of invincibility about Old Trafford; you just thought no one could touch us, and anything you did would come off. It was a lovely feeling. I've had some games there, I'll tell you. We beat Newcastle 7–2 and I got four. I'd have got five, six, seven if they'd let me.'

While there was no question they appreciated his goals, it was clear which side his team-mates quickly lined up on in the great Gordon-Hill-is-he-a-prat-or-what debate. 'Gordon was ideal, this cocky Cockney,' remembers Lou Macari. 'A lot of the lads thought, right we'll sort this one out.'

One of the unspoken rules of a football dressing-room is that no one brags about their achievement. Hill couldn't open his mouth without boasting how good he was. (A habit he still indulges in, incidentally. When the Manchester United magazine asked a bunch of former players to pick their United Dream Team in August 1996, he was the only player to pick himself.) It was felt that he therefore required more than the standard toes-cut-off-his-socks or Deep-Heat-in-the-jock-strap dressing-room pranks to shave his ego down to a manageable size. He needed, Macari reckoned, a big-time campaign of major practical jokes.

'The thing about him was,' recalls Macari, 'his impressions.' In the days before age rounded his face, Hilly had this long pointed chin with a comedy jut. It was a chin that suggested one thing above all others: Bruce Forsyth.

'Oh yeah, I used to do Brucie,' Hill explained. 'You know, I'd come off the pitch after a match, into the dressing-room and go [affects not a particularly close approximation to the master of the game show] "good game, good game". I had me Max Bygraves, and me John Waynes. But the one that went down particularly well was me Normans. Me Norman Wisdoms.'

At one stage, Hill was almost as frequently photographed by the tabloids off the pitch in Wisdom-trademark peaked cap and ill-fitting buttoned-up jacket as he was on it in a scarlet shirt, banging in the goals. At one official banquet he did a little turn, tripping over a director's wife's handbag, taking a little prat-fall, Norm-style.

'I used,' Hill recalled, 'to stick me head round the corner of the dressing-room as Norman and go [affects not a particularly close approximation to the Norman Wisdom voice] "Is there a game today?". That used to go down very well, the lads would laugh a lot at that.'

'He used to think we were laughing with him,' Alex Stepney said of Hill when I interviewed him for the *Family Tree* programme. 'We weren't. We were laughing at him.'

Even Martin Buchan, the detached one, had a line or two for Hilly. For the B-side of the 1976 Cup final single, Buchan, who liked to strum his guitar, wrote a song called 'Old Trafford Blues'. It included a couplet straight from the John Toshack school of footie poetry:

Then there's Brian Greenhoff, he's got lots of skill
And he really needs it to play with Gordon Hill.

It was, though, Macari who executed big wind-ups on the little man. On one occasion the team were in Middlesbrough for an overnight stop on a Friday night and Macari dreamt up this idea to persuade Hill that he was wanted on local television, to do his Norman Wisdom. Macari hired a cabbie to call at the team's hotel on the outskirts of the town and to drop Hill outside the television studios for the interview which didn't exist. One other thing, it was 10 o'clock at night; Macari was certain he'd be greeted with a closed building and no chance of finding a cab back to the hotel.

Hill was duly summoned by the hotel reception, and the taxi driver, playing his part in the prank to the full, took him to the studios. But this was where the joke fell flat. Hill arrived, walked into the building and was sent by a confused security guard to the local radio studio. Seeing a star footballer land unannounced on the premises, the producer put him on air immediately and Hill kept Teesside entertained with his Normans, his John Waynes and his Max Bygraves.

'When I got back to the hotel they were all waiting,' recalls Hill. 'They was all going, "How'd it go then?" And I'm going: "Didn't you hear me then, star of stage and screen?" And they all goes: "Ah no you never," and then they all pissed off to bed. You see they couldn't take the piss out of me, because I could take the piss better than any of them. Thing was, we were 11, 12, 15 different personalities. We may not have got on with each other off the pitch, we may have hated each other. But the minute we went out there on the park, we performed together like we was best of mates.'

Throughout Hill's first season, mates wasn't in it; they played like they were the 11 musketeers: one for all and all for one. Immersed, after their hiatus in the second division, in the best habit of all – winning – Doc's United stormed back into the A stream. That season, the average home attendance was the second-highest in United history at 54,750. And no wonder. At one stage there was a chance of a double but, more than that, Doc's team with Hill to the fore played with grace and danger, those attributes we expected of a proper United. In the crowd, exhausted by five years of failure, we couldn't believe it. 'Hello, Hello, United are back,' we chanted to the Gary Glitter tune. In March, we even sang 'United, United, top of the league,' as we led the division, heights so vertiginous, so unthought-of two years previously, it's a wonder we didn't all get nose-bleeds. In April, Jon and I went to Hillsborough for the FA Cup semi-final against Derby and bounced around the terrace in the Leppings Lane end, circumnavigating it in the surge, chanting: 'Just like a team that's gonna win the FA Cup, we shall not be moved.'

There was a moment in that game which seemed to sum up United in that era. On the fringes of United's box, Sammy McIlroy tangled with Derby's Bruce Rioch, until recently all blazer and respectability at Highbury. As the ball broke away, McIlroy was on the ground. Rioch placed his knee on the small of McIlroy's back and then, grabbing him by his then-copious thatch, rubbed his face into the turf. When Rioch stood up, McIlroy bounced up by his side, looked at him as if he didn't quite understand what Rioch was trying to do, shrugged his shoulders and ran off, smiling. Men against boys. Cynicism against free expression. Bad against good. Hill scored both that day: one an outrageous, banana-bending free kick, taken from so far out Derby didn't even bother constructing a proper wall; the other a jink, a dummy, a dipping 25-yarder.

I had a date that night with a girl. I rang her when we got back from Hillsborough, glowing, and said sorry, I couldn't go out, I had to watch *Match of the Day*. She said that was all right, she'd come round to my place, she liked football (not strictly true: it transpired she was a City fan). My parents were out, we watched the match ('Hill,' screamed Barry Davies, 'brilliantly struck') and then I lost my virginity in front of a rerun of that afternoon's Grand National. It was what you call a win double.

Much was expected of United that Cup final. They'd lit up the league, falling in the end to Liverpool by four points. And now they were playing Southampton, the second division benevolent home, the place Laurie McMenemy used to invite old-timers for a last hurrah on the south coast. Jim McCalliog, Peter Osgood, Peter Rodrigues – United's baby legs would run rings round them, we reckoned. As for Hill, he'd destroy them.

That was the theme in the tabloids all week, too. Snap-shots of the Doc posing with Hill and Coppell carrying shot-guns filled the back pages. Hill was interviewed everywhere, giving a bit of himself to anyone who'd ask, doing Norman Wisdom impressions for the BBC cameras the morning of the game. There was no way, Jon and I thought as we bummed a lift off a mate and his mum to Wembley, that Hill would score less than half a dozen. We brought along a bottle of sherry for our driver as a thank-you (she looked a sherry-drinker) and, in a sort of pre-emptive celebration, we'd drunk it by Keele services. That's how confident we were.

And then we stood, on our extravagantly heeled shoes, at the top of the terrace at Wembley, and watched our first Cup final disappear before our eyes. We blinked in disbelief as United faded, as Bobby Stokes scored from a position so far offside he was in Hertfordshire, as Peter Rodrigues, surely the oldest man ever to perform the feat, tottered to the royal box and held up the Cup. As for Hill, he limped out of it, substituted half-way through by David McCreery, looking lost and frightened. It was men against boys. Cynicism against free expression. Bad against good.

'There are no excuses,' said Hill, a generation on from that dismal day. 'None at all. I had a stinking game. I had my final at the semi. On the day, I was totally knackered. I was drained emotionally. Wembley, it's a very draining place. Funnily enough, the Tuesday after the Cup final we played Man City at Old Trafford and I had a fantastic game; I scored twice. But it was a bit late.'

Unlike pop stars who struggle with their difficult second album, Hill found his second season at Old Trafford much like his first. Easy. His relationship with Steve Coppell was picked up by the papers: Doc's flying wingers. In truth, they had no relationship. The cerebral and hard-working Coppell was generally a whole pitch away from the mercurial Hill, by now known in the press as Merlin (or presumably Merls, or maybe Merly).

'It just so happened Stevie was a worker, I was an entertainer,' recalled Hill. 'We played 4–2–4, it used to scare the crap out of people. But whereas Stevie used to tear back, I'd stay up. See, my philosophy was you can't score if you're not up front. There was never really a relationship.'

Nevertheless, the pair were forever linked in the public mind by a big commercial endorsement, a rarity in an era when football was regarded as the pursuit of the pariah. It came from Gillette, who used them to advertise their new G2 blade under the copy-line 'The Old One-Two', which was somewhat fanciful as they had rarely even exchanged passes, never mind performed a one-two. Coppell was approached first by the company's advertising agency, who thought his image perfect for their product: it was, well, clean-cut. Coppell told Michael Crick for his book *Manchester United: The Betrayal of a Legend* what happened next.

'As it was the first commercial deal I had been involved in, I thought I had better obtain permission and advice from my manager. I took the letter with me to show him and he told me to leave it with him and he would look into it. A week later he had sorted it all out, but it was no longer just me, but now Gordon Hill, Tommy Docherty and me. Doc, inevitably, was the star of the show and it was his car boot that was full of razors and blades rather than mine.'

Doc's version of events is somewhat different. 'They came to me,' he told me, 'and said they had this idea for me to do an ad. So I said, let's get Gordon and Stevie in on it – they'd be glad of the fee – and call it the old one-two, you know the football term. It was all my idea.'

Hill didn't really know what was going on, but did it anyway. 'Cor, it was freezing that day,' he remembered. 'We did it up in the television gantry at Old Trafford and it was freezing. They did so many takes, I got so cold I couldn't move me jaw by the end of it. Stiff it was, what with the laughing and the cold. But that's the kind of laugh you had with the Doc. It was, well, the happiest days of my life.'

Hill was precisely the kind of player Docherty favoured: fast, fluent, young and malleable. Also not given to intellectual curiosity about the boss's methods and practices. 'He was fantastic,' Hill said of the Doc. 'I know some people had their problems, but for me he was the greatest. He used to come into the dressing-room before a game and screw their team sheet up in front of you and just throw it away. That was enough motivation for you. See, he let you know that he wasn't worried about them, he was more worried about what you might do to them. He used to say: "Don't worry about them, let them worry about us."'

And Doc was particularly indulgent about his favourite's defending phobia: let someone else worry about that. Some of Hill's team-mates were less patient. Martin Buchan remembers in lurid detail the match at Old Trafford against Coventry City on 15 January 1977.

'There was this guy played for Coventry called Alan Green, 5ft 6ins, had a beard, very quick. He took the ball at me near the half-way line and I shepherded him all the way down the touchline to the goal-line. He couldn't get past me, couldn't get a cross in, so he went back to the half-way line; like a good sheep-dog I took him there. Gordon was standing beside their right full-back, Mick Coope. Coope thinks: "If I make a run, Green can give me the ball." Now Gordon looks at Coope, sees him beginning to move and thinks: "Well, I'm not going to chase him." And Coope's away and gets the ball off Green. All what I thought was my good work was being ruined. So I ran past Gordon and clipped him round the ear and said: "Why don't you waken up?"'

It was a moment which silenced Old Trafford: 55,000 people open-mouthed at the sight of reds scrapping among themselves. 'I raced back into the penalty area and actually managed to head the cross away,' continues Buchan. 'And Gordon comes up to me in his best Norman Wisdom voice and says: "Do that again and I'll kick you in the bollocks."'

'I thought it was one of them,' Hill told me. 'When I found out it was Martin, then I saw red. I went up to him and I told him if he did it again I'd kill him. The ref came over and told us to quieten down. He said he'd never sent off two blokes from the same side before and he didn't want to start now. Unfortunately the Doc wasn't there that day, and Frank Blunstone was in charge and it got in all the papers. He would've sorted it all out okay, Doc would.'

In-fighting or not, a year after his Wembley nightmare, Hill was back, facing Liverpool. Once again his goals had got United to the final. Once again he featured heavily in the BBC's Cup final preamble, making cheesy jokes about razors with the Doc in the team hotel, killing himself laughing, lying on the treatment table being massaged by Laurie Brown while reading a tabloid and remarking to Brown, with unconscious prescience given the events about to unfold: 'Cor, look at this, gaffer gets everywhere, dunnee.'

And to complete the symmetry from the previous year, once again during the game he was taken off, giving him the unenviable record of being the only man to be substituted twice in Cup finals. 'Yeah, but I had a better game,' he said. 'Though I felt very tired, I came off more for tactical reasons. We were winning 2–1 and the gaffer put David McCreery on to hold things a little tighter.'

Hold things a little tighter: not a Hill trait, that one.

Standing on the top of the open-topped bus the next day, driving to the town hall, showing the FA Cup to the hundreds of thousands in Albert Square, shoulder to shoulder with the Doc, Hill thought he had died and gone to heaven. And then, two months later, his mentor, the man who indulged his defensive incapabilities, was gone: sacked for getting everywhere with Mr Brown's wife.

'The Boss seemed to have this self-destruct button he'd press every three years,' said Hill. 'He'd build up something good, then he'd blow it. But still I was shocked. I thought: "Oh my God, who's coming in now?" Then I heard it was Sexton and I thought: "Oh no." Because he had a habit of destroying what was good. You see all he had to do was leave well alone and things would have been great for him. But he didn't.'

Nice bloke he might be, but Dave Sexton is not remembered with the affection he deserves in the stands at Old Trafford. And that is mainly due to one reason: he is the man who sold Gordon Hill.

Hill was not a Sexton player. Sexton wanted someone who might contribute a bit at the back, might tackle occasionally, might do something more than simply hang around the edge of the box hoping for delicious volleys. Jimmy Nicholl, United's right-back, had the easiest job in the club playing behind Steve Coppell; Arthur Albiston, at left-back, must have come off after most games exhausted. Sexton wanted someone who would do those things (the word he used was 'pull his weight') rather more than he wanted a phenomenal goal-scorer whose shimmies and volleys made us on the terrace reckon the admission money was a bargain. So, less than a year after the new manager arrived, despite the fact he scored 17 goals in 36 games that season, Gordon Hill was sold by Sexton for £250,000 and Mickey Thomas was bought for £300,000. For the extra £50,000 Thomas scored 11 goals in 90 games in his United career. Nothing sums up the Sexton era more succinctly than that bit of business.

'I never worked out his tactics. He was too clever; too, what's the word . . . deep,' Hill remembered. 'We had a little dispute, he told me to defend, but I couldn't do it. I got dropped, then we had talks and he said he had no plans for me in the first team. I was absolutely sick. I don't mind admitting I cried when he told me I was out. On the way home I saw someone had written on a wall near the ground "Hill in, Sexton out", so they knew, they knew in the crowd. He put me in the reserves and it happened just like it started. I was playing at Preston for the reserves and at half-time word came through that the Doc had come in for me for Derby. So they pulled me off, because they didn't want me to get injured.

'It was great that the Doc come in for me, but I was sick. I knew I wouldn't be out there on that pitch again in a red shirt. See, it was spiritual, for me. First time I scored a goal at Old Trafford I felt the ground accepted me. By the ground, I don't mean the stands or the terraces, I mean the actual ground, the turf, where all them greats had trod. I felt it saying: "You'll do for us, son." That was great, beyond words, really.

'When I went back to United with Derby, I scored. But in my own goal. Ashley [Grimes] or Macari hit a free kick, I was in the wall and it hit me in the face and went in. Afterwards I went in the United dressing-room and I said: "See, I can't help scoring here."'

For Merlin, it all went pear-shaped at Derby. The team were struggling, Docherty spent more time in court than Terry Venables and in the second game of his second season, in the League Cup at Leicester, Hill had just scored the winning goal in the match when he fell awkwardly after an innocuous challenge. His knee popped, and he was out of the game for 18 months, his ligaments shattered. When he returned, fitfully with QPR, then lucratively in America, the injury proved to have stolen his pace. His defensive disinclinations became ever more of a liability. He ended up, this man who had sent us into raptures that day at Hillsborough in the spring of 1976, playing in 1990 for Radcliffe Borough. Now all he has left of that time, that glorious time at the centre of things, is the chat.

'I can't complain how it turned out,' he said. 'I had three and a bit years in paradise. I destroyed defenders. There was no one I feared. I'd try things others wouldn't. Sometimes I wouldn't know what trick

I was going to pull until I did it. Opposition managers used to say "don't let him get the ball". I had some great games. The semis: great. Juventus: great. Newcastle: great. I had some cracking games. I got nothing at Liverpool except a cup of tea and a shower, but I think if we'd stayed together under the Doc we'd have knocked them off their pedestal.

'See, I don't think the Old Trafford fans saw the best of me. They saw the best I produced, but not the best I know inside I was capable of, before the injury did me. I knew I could have got better if I'd stayed there. I loved it there, 60,000 fans shouting and screaming so you can't hear yourself think.

'Before every game I used to get in me kit, and sit on the toilet. And I'd look at the shirt, it was a lovely shirt then, a different red from now: richer, a more pure red. And I'd almost have to pinch myself into believing it was true. And I'd say to myself: "This is real, this is you, you're playing in George Best's shirt."

'If you've done that, it doesn't matter what you do after, does it?'

THIRTEEN YEARS AND WON
THE LOT

Bryan Robson. Life began: 10.10.81

Dave Sexton had a bit of a habit as manager of Manchester United. Whenever someone did us over at Old Trafford – which was not infrequent in his time – he tried to buy them. He put in a bid on the phone for Garry Birtles after he had looked unstoppable as Forest whacked us 4–0 at home during Christmas 1977 (we were later to discover there was a cast-iron way to stop Birtles: put him in a United shirt). He dialled up again when Gary Mabbutt's brother Kevin scored a hat-trick for Bristol City in October 1978 (quite why, when he had Andy Ritchie who would score hat-tricks every time the manager condescended to allow him in the team, only Sexton knows). And what he saw during a match at the back end of 1978 put him straight on the blower once more.

In those dreary post-Docherty days there was a particular bogey team of United's: West Bromwich Albion. They always seemed to beat us, at their place in the Cup, at Old Trafford in the league, the Baggies bagged it. But their best performance was when they came to Old Trafford on 30 December 1978. Before the match, the United programme informed us that 'a feature of the Throstles' play has been the exciting, attacking skills of their coloured forwards'. They were right. Albion won 5–3. But it wasn't close. United's efforts were leather-lunged, gutsy, try-and-salvage-some-pride-late-in-the-day goals. Theirs were sharp, full of crisp movement and clinical finish: Cunningham roasting Nicholl, Regis leaping above Brian Greenhoff as if he wasn't there. Everywhere you looked they dripped class: whiffed of it like a pricey cologne.

But in among all the talent, the man who really shone for them was a slight, bandy-legged, pigeon-toed figure in midfield, who cut down United players with tackling of such ferocity and frequency you assumed he was on piece-work: ten quid a cartilage. He could pass, too, and run and shoot. There was only one thing obviously wrong with him as he took us apart, and it wouldn't take the barber long to remove that Harpo Marx corkscrew hairdo he appeared to think was stylish.

Even Dave Sexton couldn't fail to notice Bryan Robson. After the bank holiday, he put in a bid for him. But Ron Atkinson, West Brom's substantial manager, wasn't interested. As soon as he had put down the phone, he called Robson into his office dutifully to inform him of Sexton's inquiry. 'You can forget all about that,' the Ron they called Big sneered at his young player. 'There's only one way you're going to Man U. And that's if I go there first.'

Ron Atkinson reckoned Old Trafford was the place for him: big. In the summer of 1981, he swanked up the M6 from Birmingham, flash, brash and tandoori-tanned. He demanded a Merc as a company car (it was champagne-coloured), he put a sunbed in his office at the Cliff (Clayton Blackmore used to sneak in there after hours) and gave the press his home phone number ('just don't call me when *The Sweeney*'s on'). After Dave Sexton had been axed, sacked because his team hadn't won anything and were so boring they could hardly fill a sandwich never mind a stadium, Martin Edwards was looking for an entertainer. Not because he was partial to entertainment for its own sake, you understand, but because it tends to be a more saleable commodity than stodge and caution. Atkinson persuaded the chairman entertainment was his middle name and marched into his first press conference in a custard-coloured suit to prove it. Sure, Atkinson was fourth on Edwards's summer shopping list. But, hell, Ron fancied himself. There was a gag doing the rounds at the time concerning a new arrival in heaven inquiring of St Peter who the geezer in the trench coat, shades and wrap-over hair was. 'That's God,' came the reply, 'thinks he's Ron Atkinson.' And when it came to football, the Big One really fancied himself. He reckoned he was better than Laurie McMenemy, Bobby Robson and Ron Saunders put together, and here was the place to prove it.

There was no better way of insuring he made his name at Old Trafford than by bringing along in his luggage the 24-year-old midfielder who, he believed (and he is no mean judge of a player), was the best he had ever seen: Bryan Robson. Thus Big Ron's first action as manager at United was to ring his old employers. At first they were no more enthusiastic to sell Robson than Ron had been when he was in charge. After all their manager had just left them in the lurch, they'd recently sold Len Cantello and Laurie Cunningham, the last thing they needed was to explain to the fans that they were prepared to let their one-man spine go. 'Bryan Robson,' said chairman Bert Millichip (yeah, him), 'is not available at any price.' Then Ron mentioned £1.5 million, a British record fee, plus another £500,000 for Remi Moses and Millichip realised how petty and selfish he was being, standing in the way of a young player's ambitions. 'It may seem a lot of money,' said Atkinson at the press conference announcing Robbo's signing. 'But it's not a gamble, you know. You're not even gambling with someone like him. This fella is solid gold.'

If anyone knew about the value of gold it was Ron: he was wearing at the time a signet ring the size of a small satellite dish. But he was right: Robson was worth twice the money. And as for Moses, whatever Tommy Docherty might have said at the time – 'Half a million for Moses? You could get the original Moses and the tablets for that price' – he wasn't a bad prospect either. The purchase of the pair was the best thing Ron ever did. And he did it two months after he arrived. It was downhill from there.

In 1992 Bryan Robson was awarded an MA by Manchester University. Of all the honorary gongs handed out by the institution, this was the most deserved. Robbo was a master of the following arts: passing, shooting, tackling, heading, winning the ball in his own box one minute, arriving in the opposition's like the 8.30 from Piccadilly the next. Oh, and giving linesmen the full benefit of his advice while standing six inches from his ear. As if that wasn't enough, he was also a leader of men in the Alexander-the-Great class. Where Robbo went, you followed (usually into Pat Crerand's pub, but that's another story).

You got a sense of the scale of Bryan Robson during Euro 96. Before matches, as Terry Venables's right-hand man, he would wander among the England players as they warmed up on the pitch, having words, chivvying some with a clenched fist, relaxing others with an arm round the shoulder. As he approached, the players would become aware of him; they would defer to him, like young lions respecting the ravaged pride-leader in their midst. Among footballers Bryan Robson has a presence. It is a presence born of respect for his courage, his passion, his accomplishment. It is a presence which meant that when, as a fresh, new player-manager of no experience, he flew to São Paulo, he could persuade the best young player in Brazil to sign for Middlesbrough. He persuaded the top young Brazilian to play for Middlesbrough: repetition does not dull that achievement. And Juninho said the moment he met Bryan Robson, never mind the cash promised by Barcelona and Benfica, he knew he wanted to play for Middlesbrough.

Robson achieves all this without any braggadocio. Despite his celebrity, he remains a friendly, decent, undemonstrative bloke. When you first talk to him, if you didn't know who he was, you would think him barely capable of ordering a beer, never mind persuading a top South American to play on Teesside. He possesses one of the least compelling speaking voices in public life: a soft, impenetrable, Geordie monotone that rivals the late-night shipping forecast in its ability to solve insomnia. In fact, you think, when you speak to him, it must have been that Juninho misheard, and thought he said Milan.

Thus the Bryan Robson who arrived at Old Trafford in the autumn of 1981 was a markedly different proposition from the colossus – the only man in history to lift the FA Cup three times – that his future exploits made him. That Bryan Robson, diffident, unsophisticated, a Geordie lad in a perm, not quite fitting his new suit, almost filled his pants at the thought of what lay ahead.

'It was a big gamble for Ron, paying that much money for me,' Robson said, when I spoke to him in an executive box overlooking the Cellnet Riverside Stadium at the end of his second season in management. 'I think a lot of people in the Old Trafford boardroom must have looked at one another and said: "Bryan who?" And what I found was a massive club. People talk about your Arsenals, your Tottenhams, your Liverpools, but United are truly massive.'

It wasn't so much the stadium, or the overwhelming interest of the press, or the expectation of the fans that made him appreciate

Manchester United were a bigger operation than he was used to, that made him realise what he was dealing with. It was more the little touches. He was amazed by the fact the club provided players with flip-flops and bath-robes in the changing-rooms, the way that in the players' lounge the drinks were free after games, whereas at West Brom you had to dip in your pocket, which was a bit much after you'd just risked sinews in their cause. This was a place, he thought, big enough to care.

And his nerves in those first few days were not helped by Ron's insistence that the signing of his contract, instead of being conducted in the privacy of the boardroom, or even at a press conference in front of a couple of dozen snappers taking a moment out from assaulting the free coffee and sandwiches, was to be done more publicly. Ron, you see, was an entertainer. He and Martin Edwards wanted to make a point that the shy and retiring Sexton days were over: the big new record signing would put his name on the dotted line out on the pitch at Old Trafford. Before a home match. In front of 46,837 people.

So a table was set up on the apron of the pitch around which sat manager and chairman. Also a player giving a passable impression of a condemned man on his way to the gallows. 'It was very embarrassing,' the captain later to be known as Marvel recalled. 'I didn't want to do it like that at all, but Ron egged us on. He said it was the chairman's idea, though I think the chairman said it was Ron's idea. We were playing Wolves and after we'd done it, I sat in the stand and watched Sammy McIlroy, who everyone surmised was going to be left out of the team for me, score a hat-trick. So it was all very strange. I think sometimes with a big fee for a player, people think it's you what gets the one and a half million or whatever, not the club. You get the pressure because it's all new. It's not as though anyone can have warned you, educated you as to what to expect. It's all new. And I would have hated to be the £1.5 million flop.'

There was plenty of precedent that he might. Steve Daley, across town at City, had recently suffered horrors at the hands of a fee not much less than Robson's. So poor were Daley's performances it was widely assumed City's owner Peter Swales must have been operating some complicated tax loss adjustment when he paid £1.25 million for him. There had to be some explanation.

But with Robson, nerves or not, there was never any doubt. The moment he stepped on the pitch for his debut on 10 October 1981 against Manchester City at Maine Road you thought, he'll do. The team that day was: Bailey, Gidman, Albiston, Wilkins, Moran, Buchan, Robson, Birtles (Coppell), Stapleton, McIlroy, Moses; the score was 0–0; the crowd 52,037. Robson wasn't flash, or cocky, or one to humiliate an opponent with a nutmeg. He didn't have a particularly athletic physique. What he had was a quality his colleagues spotted from the off. There he was, arriving in the dressing-room, teacher's pet, the most expensive player in British football, bound to take someone's place and yet they loved him. 'The moment he walked in, you could see what we had on our hands,' says Lou Macari. 'A player of immense power.'

They loved him because they knew, in the midfield of an English league team as in trench warfare, you want someone alongside you who you can be certain will go over the top. Preferably on Graeme Souness. 'Sometimes with him,' remembers Gordon McQueen, 'the rest of the team could say: "come on, skip, win it for us." There's not many you can ask that of.'

What Robson had, beneath that quiet demeanour and bad hair, was the most advanced will to win in British football. He showed that in his junior career, when, as a young player at WBA he had suffered three broken legs as he put himself in places that his physique was unwilling to follow, and yet forced himself to recover and to get better each time – drinking a cocktail of Guinness, sherry and raw eggs to build his physique. He showed it when you watched him during games, as he clenched his jaws together so hard you thought he was going to grind his teeth into powder. And nowhere better did you see it than on the night of 21 March 1984 in the Cup Winners' Cup quarter-final against Barcelona.

Nine months earlier, Robson had won the Cup for United. After a two-all draw against Brighton (Ray Wilkins scored a wonder goal and then knackered himself celebrating) the captain took charge of the replay. He wanted a medal badly, that's why he had come to United, and in the first game, but for a late miss by Gordon Smith, Brighton would have denied him. He wasn't taking any further chances, and in the replay he destroyed the Seagulls (not the ones who followed the trawlers), scoring twice and hammering them with his tackles. Four–nil it was, and he lifted the trophy like a man possessed.

He saw that triumph as only the beginning. In the Cup Winners'
Cup the following year, the reds beat Dukla Prague (complete with
away kit) and Spartak Varna (who? Exactly!) before drawing
Barcelona in the quarter-final. The first leg at the Nou Camp was
lost 2–0. No one seemed particularly surprised. Barcelona had Diego
Maradona and Bernd Schuster; United had Mike Duxbury and
Arthur Albiston. But what Barca didn't have was Bryan Robson.
Sometimes, football is advanced by individual acts of determination
and courage rather than by broader visions of tactics and strategy.
The second leg of that game, the night of 21 March 1984, was such
an occasion. Robson brushed aside the Spaniards in their primrose
shirts, oozing a fearsome drive which infected his colleagues, carried
them to effort previously thought impossible.

He scored the first with a header, diving full length to meet
Graeme Hogg's flick-on from a corner. He scored the second,
scooping up when the Barca keeper dropped a shot. 'Come on,' you
could see him yelling from the centre circle after that goal. 'We can
do these.' Then, as if to prove his point, he helped Frank Stapleton
to the third, at which point 58,547 fans inside Old Trafford went
barking, there were complaints about the noise from Rochdale and
Bobby Charlton danced in the directors' box ('the immense joy
resulting from that victory surpassed anything I have ever
experienced in the game,' Sir Bob said the next day, as if scripted by
the speech bubble writer from 'Billy The Fish'). Those who were
there realised that never, in a history of glitter and polish, has Old
Trafford witnessed an individual performance like it. Barca were
routed. Maradona, not one to forget a slight, got his revenge over
England two years later with a hand from God.

When it was over, hundreds of overexcited casuals scaled the
fences and joyfully chaired Robson on their shoulders (the police
were too exercised by the thrill of the game to stop them). The set
of Robbo's face as he was carried away told it all. Not a Gazza smirk
of triumph, but cold-eyed, jaw clenched, chin jutting, still seized
with the effort of will. Either that, or he was just terrified the lads
were trying to take him away to be flogged on the black market. He
was, after all, the most valuable thing any of them had ever
touched.

Soon after the Barca match, Juventus put in a bid for Robson.
Ron Atkinson called him into his office once more to inform him

of transfer interest from another club. 'I've told them, there's no way you're going, skipper, for less than three million,' sneered Ron.

In 1996, £3 million will land you a pedestrian full-back. In 1984, it would have been a world-record fee. 'There was no way anybody was prepared to pay that for me,' remembered Robson. 'I think Ron knew that.'

He was right. Ron wasn't going to let Robson go: he knew the player was good at West Brom, and he had grown immeasurably since he had arrived at Old Trafford. Though the two would clash titanically ('I've never been the type of person who can sit in the dressing-room at half-time and keep my mouth shut and accept things,' Robson told me. 'And Ron had this habit of always blaming me and Ray Wilkins every time we lost'), the Big Man loved having a player like that in his team. It was the same for England. Robson's namesake, Bobby, used to lose all dignity at the mere mention of the Captain Marvel moniker, eyes dampening, words slurring, love oozing from every pore.

'He was three players in one,' Bobby wrote of Bryan in his book, *Against All Odds*. 'A defender, a midfielder and a phenomenal goal-scorer. He was dominant in set-plays at both ends. Maybe I'm biased, but I could see no failings. England were a taller, prouder team when he played.'

In the dressing-room, too, Robson was not the sort of captain who believed his duties began and ended with sorting out the freebie tickets. When Norman Whiteside arrived in the first team, Robson took the 16-year-old aside and advised him to get some insurance.

'Why would a kid like me need insurance?' Whiteside asked.

'Trust me,' Robbo replied. 'You might.'

Sadly, he did.

Gordon Strachan remembers he was barely through the door at Old Trafford before he and his wife were invited round to the Robsons' for Sunday lunch, where they were told where the nice places to live were. And by the end of his career, Robson was acting as a sort of manager's assistant, offering advice from the dug-out as he sat on the bench, playing the go-between on transfer dealings – he made first contact with Viv Anderson, for instance, sounding him out about whether he would be interested in coming to United – and spending much of his spare time watching the juniors, getting to know them, finding out who the prospects were.

'I think when you're at a club you're all in it together,' Robbo told me. 'If you've got knowledge young lads don't have, I believe you should pass that knowledge on to them.'

There was one flaw in the great man's make-up, just one characteristic preventing the Pope from canonising him on the spot as the greatest Englishman ever to kick a ball. Due to a propensity for flinging himself into places even Kevin Moran would shy away from, Bryan Robson did himself damage. Injuries: Robbo was a by-word for them. He was absent from vital games with shin and hamstring problems, he missed whole tranches of seasons with dislocations and sprains. The image of Robson many people hold is not the lion-hearted destroyer of Barcelona, but the shrunken figure stumbling off a Mexican pitch in the 1986 World Cup, flanked by alarmed-looking physios, clutching his dislocated shoulder. And in many quarters it is this image which has led to Robson's career being post-rationalised as a failure. For instance, when George Best was asked to pick his favourite team of all time for the BBC2 show celebrating his 50th birthday, he included, because he of all people knows a thing or two about what constitutes a great player, Bryan Robson. The panel brought together by the show to analyse the choice scoffed at Robson's inclusion as evidence that booze had finally addled old Bestie's brain.

'England wasted so much time thinking he might get fit,' said one.

'He's presumably only in there out of United solidarity,' said another.

'Anyway,' said a third. 'He wouldn't be able to play. He'd pull a hamstring walking from the dressing-room.'

Robson and injuries, they were pretty inseparable. They went together like, well, Robson and Jerome. 'You know,' the man himself said to me. 'I've been a lot more fortunate than a lot of players with injuries.'

You what? You, fortunate? The man who was cut down every time he stood on the brink of something huge, the man who, had he stayed fit, would have come close to overtaking Bobby Charlton's record number of appearances in a United shirt.

'People talk about my injuries, but I have still played about 800 senior games, which is a lot more than some lads. Okay, I had some injuries. But they were highlighted because of when and where they've been. I missed two World Cups through them, I missed a League Cup final, I missed the run-in to the championship in 1992. But if those injuries had been at the start of the season, or the middle, no one would have noticed.'

There was, though, one other aspect to his absence through injury. It diminished the team disproportionately. To remove the player who combined engine, drive, heart and inspiration from the side was to weaken it beyond simple remedy. Too often for United and England there was a sense of 'if only Robbo were playing' and 'it'll all be sorted when Robbo gets back'. This is not to belittle his achievement: he is United's longest-serving captain (at 12 years); he holds the record of scoring in 20 consecutive league seasons; when he scored against Oldham Athletic in the FA Cup semi-final replay in 1994 (with what, frankly, can only be described as a groin-poke) at 37 years 92 days he became the oldest man since the war to put the ball in the net for United. No, what it suggests was that, under Ron Atkinson and in the early Ferguson years, United were over-reliant on him. A prime example was 1985: United won the first ten games of the season, looked to be cantering to the title, then Robson was injured in the 12th and didn't play again until the spring, by which time the team was lucky to be fourth. Such was his dominance, such was his influence, that when he was absent there was no system to cope. It was, in short, a one-man team.

'I don't think you ever have one man who is a team. It is a team game and we had a lot of good players at United at that time,' the man himself suggested. 'The way Ron worked, though, he had this circle he was interested in, that he devoted all his energies to. Which worked well for the players in it. But the fringe players felt left out a bit and Ron's banter sometimes wasn't the best for them. And when you got injuries that's when it showed, because the fringe players always felt, well I'm coming in for a couple of games, but it doesn't matter how well I'm doing, I'll be left out again. Also in a team you need stronger players as well as gifted ones. You need someone to win the ball for your Strachans and Olsens and Wilkinses. When I was out mebbes the squad wasn't deep enough, mebbes weaker players come in and mebbes the whole team was wanting a little bit in midfield.'

In November 1986, Ron Atkinson was sacked from Manchester United. Not many at the club were surprised, least of all Atkinson

himself. The Big Man seemed to lose heart after the team he had
built blew the title the previous season. His hold on the club had
slipped, discipline was poor and if he had bought some of his recent
purchases at Marks and Spencer he would have been entitled to take
them back and demand a refund ('I'm returning a Sivebaek, a
Barnes, a Higgins and two Gibsons please'). And when Robson
returned from the Mexico World Cup and booked straight into
hospital to have his shoulder attended to by a jigsaw puzzle expert,
Ron knew he was a gonner. As he left, heading for Spain, many
people expected Robson to go with him. The two had been so closely
identified, father and son, and the new manager might have other
plans, his own boys to bring in. But such an analysis was to
underestimate Bryan Robson. This time round it was Ron receiving
rather than giving out the disappointing news about Robbo
availability: there was no way he was leaving.

'You feel you have let the manager down when he gets the sack,'
Robson said of his mentor's departure. 'Because if you are a player at
a club and the manager gets sacked it is because of poor
performances. And I think at that time all the players had to look at
themselves a little bit.'

Robson believed he had let the club down, too. To walk off in the
manager's wake was thus to relinquish his responsibilities. Besides, in
his five years at Old Trafford, he had fallen in love with the place and
he had become overwhelmed by the romance of Manchester United.
His own ambition was hypercharged, but it matched exactly the
ambition of the club. He had always wanted to win a championship
medal more than anything; now he wanted to win one with
Manchester United. 'Even when we won the Cup,' he said, 'you
sensed it wasn't good enough. What we all wanted was the
championship.'

The sad irony of Bryan Robson is that when a team befitting his
talents and capable of landing the one he craved was constructed, he
could do little more than flit on its peripheries. It wasn't that Alex
Ferguson didn't want to include him. Like all Robson's other
managers, almost as soon as he arrived at Old Trafford, Fergie fell
under the Marvel's spell. 'You only have to study Bryan Robson to
discover the right attitude,' the manager wrote in his book, *The First
Six Years*. 'Isn't he a joy to behold? How he bursts himself to win
games.'

No, it was simply that there was one enemy Robson couldn't overcome: time. The three and a half years Ferguson took to get into gear was time Robson could ill afford. And even then, though the FA Cup in 1990 was a treat, and the Cup Winners' Cup in 1991 an unexpected bonus (he missed the 1992 Rumbelows Cup through, you've guessed it, injury), the championship would take a little longer. In 1992, as United crumbled within touching distance of the prize, Robson's absence from nine of the last 13 league matches was all they needed: injury had got him again.

And by 1993 Ferguson, recognising what his predecessors could not bear to face, realised if the championship was to be won, he couldn't wait for Robson. Cantona was bought, McClair moved back to midfield to partner Ince and the Marvel only appeared five times. But significantly, for the last nine games in the run-in, he was substitute. Ferguson realised that, even if the legs didn't have the power anymore, his desire, his passion, his will could still serve a purpose. In that title run-in, with Aston Villa flaking, Robson would pace the touchline during matches, yelling out instructions, bawling words of encouragement, stiffening resolves from 30 yards. 'You need good players with strong minds if you are going to achieve things,' he told me. And from the touchline, he was there to make sure minds were concentrated.

The night the title was won, when Villa were overcome by mathematics and Oldham at home, Robson, with the rest of the team, went to Steve Bruce's house for a celebratory half-dozen. In the morning, with United due to face Blackburn that afternoon, Bruce awoke bleary eyed to the sound of clinking. Wandering down to the kitchen, he discovered Robbo and his wife, Denise, had cleared up the entire place. That's what you call taking responsibility. Bruce probably remembered that, remembered the contribution Robson had made over the years, remembered the contribution he had made over the previous six weeks from his position in the dug-out, and when it was time to lift the ugly weight of silver that was the new Premiership trophy, the new captain insisted the old one came with him.

'Brucie said I should pick up the trophy with him,' remembered Robson. 'At first I declined; he deserved the honour on his own. But him and Alex were adamant. It was a good thing for them to do.' Robson's United career had come full circle, closing as it had opened with a grand gesture on the Old Trafford turf.

The following week United, crowned champions for the first time in 26 years, were at Wimbledon. I took my son along on his fifth birthday, expecting nothing more than a stroll, an exhibition in the south London sun. If that was the case, someone had neglected to inform Robbo. Early in the second half, he burst through Wimbledon's offside trap and, as the whole of Selhurst Park, decorated red, white and black for the day, willed it to happen, he scored. Vinny Jones went apoplectic. It was a mean-nothing, end-of-season stroll, but Jones ran full pelt at the linesman, screaming invective. You might call that will to win. But there was a difference with Robson: he had the skill to execute that will. While Vinny Jones complained about goals, Robbo scored them.

It was widely expected Robson would leave that summer. But Alex Ferguson needed him to do a job in the European Cup. The UEFA rule restricting the number of foreigners in a team (and classifying Welsh, Irish and Scotsmen as foreigners) meant he could never field his strongest team in the competition. Even at 36, limbs ravaged by effort, Robson would be an asset. I went on the plane to Budapest for the first-round match against Honved with the team. While the other players spent the flight sleeping, or playing cards, or flicking rolled-up pieces of paper at the heads of those that slept, Robson was busy organising events for his Scanner Appeal, which raised a couple of million for a Manchester children's hospital. (Charity work, too; has the man no down-side?) 'It all started,' he explained, 'when I visited the hospital next to the Cliff. It sort of put it all into perspective, really, everything I had but they didn't have.'

There wasn't much charity around in United's return to the trophy the pursuit of which once killed the entire team. Galatasaray were criminally underestimated at Old Trafford (three of their team that night – Tugay, Turkylmaz and Hakan – played in Euro 96 compared to two of United's – Schmeichel and Ince). In Istanbul, United made an embarrassed, woeful exit, compounded by Robson needing three stitches in a hand wound after being assaulted by a Turkish policeman.

If the romantics felt it was only appropriate that Robson went out at Old Trafford, they were to have their wish fulfilled. Once again United won the league, and once again, though he had only appeared ten times in the campaign, Steve Bruce called him to lift the Premiership trophy. He had played in the last league match of the season like a novice, with a point to prove. While everyone else strolled, he stretched and galloped and charged, desperate to score his 100th goal for the club. In the last couple of minutes I thought he was going to do it, thought the script was tailored to the legend. He was lurking outside the area, the action seemed to slow, as it does just before a goal, he struck it clean and fresh. And it missed by an inch.

A week later, it was the Cup final. Robson had come into an injury and suspension crisis in the semi and played, brilliantly. He wanted to play in the final; he thought he should have played in the final; it would have been just right if he had. But Alex Ferguson was never one to let sentiment get in the way of the need to win. He knew his best team and Robbo wasn't in it. Not even on the bench.

'I said to him: "You're going to be a manager soon, what would you do?"' Ferguson recalled. 'And he said: "Play myself."'

Robson left Old Trafford, bound for Middlesbrough and management, with six major medals in the cabinet of his Cheshire home: two championships ('92–'93, '93–'94); three FA Cup ('83, '85, '90); one European Cup Winners' Cup ('91). This places him fifth in the all-time list of United winners. Those above him? Not Law, Best, Charlton, Foulkes or Carey. But Mark Hughes, Brian McClair and Steve Bruce in second place with seven. And at the top Gary Pallister with eight.

Robson took with him a knowledge, gleaned from Atkinson and Ferguson, of how a team should be managed (and in one or two aspects should not). In his first year, his team, playing quick-witted, bright, intelligent football, was promoted. And, back in the Premiership on his return to Old Trafford in the autumn of 1995, he was given a reception so huge it was like that night against Barcelona all over again.

'It didn't surprise me,' said the new manager of the welcome. 'United fans have always been brilliant to me. But I think it shocked some of my players. They just stood in the middle of the pitch and wondered what the hell had happened. They couldn't play for the first five minutes.'

It was a greeting that suggested the crowd were looking forward to a time when they might see him at Old Trafford on a regular basis once more, as successor to Alex Ferguson when he decides to retire. 'I don't know about that,' Robson said when I asked him if he ever fancied the job. 'As I said when I made myself unavailable for the England job, I've got a fantastic club here, a fantastic chairman and a big job to do. I'm not going to walk away from this.'

Walk away in the middle of a job: Bryan Robson is no more likely to do that than he is to walk away in the middle of a pint. But that's another story.

FEET FIRST

Norman Whiteside. Life began: 15.5.82

On 9 February 1986 Ron Atkinson stepped off the Manchester United team coach as it arrived outside the players' entrance at Anfield, put his head down and prepared to run the gauntlet. He could usually rely on a reception at Liverpool's ground: the odd ripe insult, a hay-maker or two swung in his direction through the police cordon, not to mention gob – showers of the stuff – buggering up his match-day suit. But what he got on this occasion, he wasn't prepared for. As he made his way, head down, through the welcoming committee, something horrible hit him in the eyes and mouth, an acrid, foul-tasting, cloying gack. He staggered through the players' entrance into the corridor beyond, rubbing at his eyes, yelling, scattering a poor by-stander who was in his way, thrusting him aside in his dash for self-preservation.

There were two things Ron Atkinson learnt after he'd run into the nearest washroom, stuck his head in a sink-full of water and eased the burning pain in his face. The first was that football thuggery had taken a new turn: he had been attacked by a Liverpool supporter flourishing a CS canister and had got a face-full of gas. And the second was that the man he had unceremoniously flung against the wall in his panic was his new signing, the Danish international John Sivebaek, who that afternoon was due to make his debut. A great introduction to English football, that: assaulted by your manager who'd just been gassed.

'Sometimes it was like Vietnam, Man U–Liverpool,' Ron once told me. 'It was nasty. It wasn't hostile, it was hatred.'

He was right. In the mid-'80s no one loathed each other like United and Liverpool. As a United fan visiting Anfield you learnt that Stanley Park was named in memory of the bloke who invented the craft knife. And Liverpool fans would count themselves lucky if their coaches escaped down the East Lancs Road from Old Trafford with one window intact. For those who wanted to bundle, the city centre meets after matches carried a wholly disproportionate edge.

It had been going on a long time, this inter-city rivalry, a hatred born of proximity, an ancient enmity between Catholic free spirit and Protestant self-belief. But by the mid-'80s it had declined down a horrible spiral. While Liverpool were unarguably the best team in the land, their fans couldn't handle the fact we remained unarguably the most glamorous; they loathed the fact that people in Timbuktu had heard of us and not them, even though we hadn't won the title for years. In turn, we hated them because they won everything in sight and taunted us hollow about it. They besmeared the memory of Munich to wind us up; we retaliated by assaulting the legacy of Shankly. It was pitiful, tiresome and, by 1986, dangerous. And it spread on to the pitch. The two teams tore into each other, knowing how much it meant to their supporters, roared on by the over-excited to acts of career-jeopardising recklessness.

But what made those mid-'80s meets particularly joyful for us was that, though Liverpool might be able to win everything, gluttonously acquiring European Cups and league championships, we were their bogey team. In Ron Atkinson's time they only beat us once. Throughout his career, Ron has always thrived on the big match, loved plotting for it, loved raising his players for it. Twice in the '90s, for instance, with Villa and Sheffield Wednesday, thanks to his planning and his inspiration, he did United in League Cup finals. In the end that was part of his undoing at Old Trafford: always great in a final, not much use on a wet Wednesday in November in the league at Southampton; the big cup sprinter, when what we needed was a marathon runner.

But, nevertheless, Liverpool against United? Ooh, he loved it, relished the fact it meant something, thrived on pitching himself against the best. And most of all he loved setting Norman Whiteside on them.

There is a scene in the film *Mad Max II* where the Humungous, Max's corpulent, masked enemy, decides enough is enough and unleashes the mad-eyed hell's angel he has hitherto kept chained to his vehicle, setting him off out into the battle. The consequences will be horrible, the Humungous suggests by his action, but things have gone beyond worrying about that. Norman was the footballing equivalent of that man: Humungous Ron's secret weapon. And nowhere did he work better than against Liverpool, in there mixing it with the Scousers.

'I played in both the Manchester derby and the Merseyside derby, which were both great,' Whiteside told me. 'But for me, it was always Man U v. Liverpool. I loved playing at Anfield. They hated me; you could hear them chanting 'Whiteside is a . . . ' whatever. But the Kop never frightened me; I loved that – it spurred me on. I thought they must have thought I was going to do something. I had a great record against them. The best players I've ever played against were Hansen and Lawrenson, but yet we got success against them. I got success against them.'

Indeed, Whiteside had an unimpeachable record against Liverpool: played 16, won 6, drew 9, lost 1 (the League Cup final in 1983), scoring four goals. His most symbolic moment in the clash of the titans, however, came not under Ron but in the early days of Alex Ferguson. He was substitute for the game at Anfield on 4 April 1988 and by the time Fergie roused his weapon from the bench to replace Colin Gibson midway through the second half, it looked a lost cause: United were 3–1 down and the Liverpool midfield were rampant. Norman, though, didn't believe in lost causes.

His first action, this man who always rose to the occasion, was to seek out Steve McMahon, Liverpool's enforcer. They met in the centre circle, they entwined limbs, Norman got up, McMahon didn't. Then he sought out Ronnie Whelan. They met in the centre circle, they entwined limbs, Norman got up, Whelan didn't. For the reds in the stands, it was just what they wanted. Inspired by this whirlwind on the pitch, they roared on United. The players too sensed the strength suddenly injected into their midst and they rallied, exploiting the holes their one-man demolition operation had made in the wall of the Liverpool side. Minutes after Norman's handiwork (or rather, footwork), Robson got his second of the game to make it 3–2. And then Strachan, fed by Davenport, homed in on the Kop end, faced up to Bruce Grobbelaar and slotted the equaliser. As 5,000 United fans went delirious, 35,000 Scousers howled their displeasure – they'd all see him outside, they reckoned. In a pretence of cool, though his guts were in his shorts at the time, Strachan celebrated by standing in front of the Kop and miming smoking a cigar. Then he turned to Whiteside and thanked him for making it all possible. And Norman, the Scouse Buster, our hero, just grinned.

'Funnily enough, people often remind me of that game,' Whiteside told me. 'I remember as soon as I came on I tackled Steve McMahon, stood on his toe, and he was out the game and we went on to get a 3–3 draw. It seems to have stuck in a lot of memories.'

Not least Steve McMahon's.

Norman Whiteside had a hell of a reputation in football: the hardest of the hard. But, like most reputations, it hid more than it revealed. Viv Anderson, for instance, remembers having completely the wrong idea about him when he joined Manchester United.

'I used to go up to Robbo at England sessions,' Anderson told me, 'and say to him: "You've got to admit, Whiteside, he's a dirty so-and-so." And Robbo would say: "No, he's a smashing lad." And I'd go: "Nah, he's filthy." Then when I signed for United, Norman came up to me first day and said: "I hear you think I'm a dirty so-and-so." And I thought: "Eh, this is going to be a bit tricky." But he turned out to be just as Robbo said he was: a lovely lad.'

And he is. Good company, funny, with a real mischievous twinkle. Off the pitch there isn't a hint of Nasty Norman. But there is something else about him and his reputation: had things gone differently, instead of being remembered as the Red Rottweiler or the Shankhill Skinhead, Norman Whiteside might have been United's Kenny Dalglish. He was that good.

The morning of the 1985 FA Cup final, I had no hope of a ticket. I thought I was going to have to watch the game on the telly. Then about 11 o'clock, in one of those moments that happen so rarely you imagine some dreadful consequence will befall you in exchange for such good fortune, my old girlfriend, Martin Buchan's old neighbour, rang to say she had a spare. It was for the Everton end, she said, so you'll have to keep quiet.

I did well. Even when Kevin Moran was sent off by Peter Willis ('Who's the Scouser in the black?' demanded the hordes at the other end of the stadium) I managed to swallow my fury. When Bryan

Robson hit his own bar with a back header from a corner in the first bit of extra time, I managed to suppress a groan. But then, in the 110th minute, my Trappist vows went down the U-bend. Jesper Olsen, playing auxiliary left-back, nodded the ball to Mark Hughes who was coming back into his own half. Hughes controlled it, turned, beat Paul Bracewell and then, with the outside of his right foot, clipped a curling pass into the feet of Norman Whiteside who, knackered by now, was out on the right wing solely because he had not tracked back from an earlier attack. Whiteside took five touches to move the ball into the edge of Everton's penalty area, where he was faced by Pat van den Hauwe. Letting the ball roll, he confused the Welshman with the Belgian name by wafting his left foot around in the air above the ball. Then he leant on to his right foot, dipped his shoulder and, with his left foot, curled the ball from 25 yards, setting it on a perfect track towards the goal. It hit the one place in the net Neville Southall hadn't covered, adding insult to injury by sending his little keeper's sponge bag spinning over and away. It seemed unreal, impossible, to beat a keeper as good as that so precisely. And for over a decade it stood as the most majestic goal I'd ever seen in a Cup final, until Eric Cantona decided he would better it.

I didn't see the Cup being presented to Bryan Robson ten minutes later. By then, several men in bad moustaches and Sergio Tacchini track pants, taking exception to my animated celebration of Whiteside's genius, had kicked me in the direction of the exit. But that evening, lying on the floor – I couldn't sit down; my arse was too bruised – I watched the whole thing again on *Match of the Day*. John Motson went as mad as I did when Whiteside scored.

'What can you say about Norman Whiteside?' Motty spluttered as Norman ran celebrating towards the United terraces. 'The youngest scorer in FA Cup final history two years ago, still only 20, writes another chapter in one of the great storybook biographies of post-war football. When they write the Norman Whiteside story, I wonder, where will they start? And, for that matter, where will they finish?'

No wonder Motty loved him; Norman was a stats-anorak's dream. His records were so prodigious they will probably never be broken: youngest-ever international in the British Isles; youngest-ever player in the World Cup finals; youngest-ever player to score in the League Cup final; youngest-ever player to score in the FA Cup final.

Norman Whiteside did everything young, including retiring. He had been finished with the game five years when United won the double at Wembley on 11 May 1996, yet he was still younger than four of the squad that day (Bruce, McClair, Pallister and Schmeichel).

Young, though, was always a bit of a misnomer for Norman Whiteside. He seemed to be born a man, to appear on the scene a fully formed, fully frightening specimen. At the age of 12 he first came to Manchester United, sent over from his home in Belfast by Bob Bishop, the man who had previously dispatched from Northern Ireland Sammy McIlroy, Jimmy Nicholl, David McCreery and, more to the point, George Best. At 14, a colossal junior centre-forward, he was signed as a schoolboy.

'Dave Sexton gave me a choice,' Norman remembered. 'I could stay in Ireland, finish my education and fly over to play for United at weekends. Or I could come over to Manchester and finish my education here. Seeing what an English education did for Gazza, I'm glad I stayed.'

Mark Hughes, 18 months older and 18 months further up the United system, recalls coming across the young Whiteside, this commuter from the Shankhill, for the first time in a schoolboy international: 'I remember the lads taking one look at the Northern Ireland team and seeing this bloody huge great skinhead lining up for them and all of us thinking: "What the hell, he must be about 25." We lost, I think he scored, the showers weren't working and the dressing-room was flooded. Not a great day.'

It wasn't long before the giant was in the first team. Ron Atkinson, by then the manager, reckoned Whiteside may have been only 16, but he was old enough for sure. So, on 24 April 1982, he came on as substitute at the Goldstone Ground against Brighton, replacing Mike Duxbury.

'Wilkins scored, and we won 1–0,' Norman remembered. 'But the biggest thing that sticks in my mind was I was on £16 a week at that time as an apprentice pro, and the win bonus was £600. So I went home with 600 quid in my pocket for playing 12 minutes of football for Man United.' Some guys get all the luck.

He made his full debut a month later against Stoke at Old Trafford on 15 May 1982. The team that day was as follows: Bailey, Gidman, Albiston, Wilkins, Moran, McQueen, Robson, Birtles (McGarvey),

Whiteside, Grimes, Coppell; the score was 2–0; the crowd 43,072. Inevitably, given the legend he was preparing, Norman scored on his debut.

A month later, barely 17, he was picked for Northern Ireland to play in the World Cup in Spain. He scored against Morocco, and contributed to Northern Ireland's greatest-ever performance, when they beat the host nation to qualify for the second stage. He was, at the time, younger than Pele had been when he first pulled on the yellow shirt of Brazil. By the time he came back from Spain his head must have been the size of an over-inflated beach ball.

'I didn't really realise what was going on,' he said. 'I went from being a schoolboy to playing in the World Cup finals overnight. I just thought it was part of my job and got on with it. I just did what I was told and played football.'

And the other players, the grown-ups in the dressing-room, how did they cope with the prodigy in their midst? 'Ninety-nine point nine per cent of footballers are just working-class lads; they treated me as another working-class lad trying to do a job. I still had to make cups of tea and turn off the telly, the little chores young apprentices are supposed to do, and that's probably a great thing.'

And the manager, how did he treat him? 'I remember when he first came up to me at the Cliff and said: "That's it, son, you're in the first team; you're in the magic circle." Which was, you know, great. You imagine, it's all you could wish for. I remember a bit later I passed my driving test, and thought I'd like a new car. I knocked on Ron's door and asked for a club car. I think he put me on an extra 100 quid a week and put me on a contract that tied me for life. He was shrewd.'

Life couldn't have been better for the young forward. The season after his debut he played 57 games, matched up front with Frank Stapleton. As well as a mature head, as well as power and strength, Whiteside had real technique, a gorgeous ability to trap the ball, to shield it from predators, to strike with both feet. It was there for all to see in the League Cup final that year against Liverpool (who else?) when he swivelled Alan Hansen and smacked in a corker. Or as he did in the FA Cup semi-final, when he made David O'Leary look flat-footed and threatened the fabric of the net with his shot. He scored the second in the Cup final replay against Brighton and went off on holiday that year with many a pundit predicting that, were he able to develop a yard of pace, he could become the best player in the world. Ron Atkinson suggested he have a beer to celebrate his arrival – he was just old enough to buy one for himself – and he liked that idea. But that's another story.

The trouble was, Norman never developed that yard of pace. As he matured, he seemed to slow down, and then he started to get into trouble. In the 1984–85 season he moved back into midfield ('the rate I'm going I'll be a centre-back, then a goalie by the time I'm 30,' he said at the time). The move was done in part to accommodate the young bull known as Mark Hughes up front, but also because Ron Atkinson felt in the middle Norman's lack of pace would be less obtrusive, and he could play to his strength and his bite. But in there, too, diving in where others feared to stamp, he was not quite quick enough to get away, and he started to get caught, both by the referee and by opponents' studs. In his first year in the middle he missed 21 games through a cocktail of knocks and bruises, particularly to his knee. He was back to spin Motty into orgasms at the 1985 Cup final, but reality was beginning to impinge on the fairy tale.

Not least in the amount he was taking home. For all its present-day money-spinning and commercial zest, football is not long out of the feudal system. If there was ever an opportunity of screwing down a player's money, it would be taken. Managers now complain about agents and about the lack of loyalty shown by star players, but it is the machismo mean streak in football's administrators that is directly responsible for both. Young players who come through the system have traditionally been paid less than incoming transfers for no better reason than the clubs think they can get away with it. It doesn't matter if they are better, have won more or done more; they present an opportunity to save money. It still goes on. When Alex Ferguson transferred Paul Ince, Andrei Kanchelskis and Mark Hughes in the summer of 1995, United's wage bill fell by ten per cent. There were over 45 professionals on the books, which suggests the new talent is not on the same income planet. Yet I don't recall the ticket prices coming down exponentially to reflect the fact we were watching players deemed less worthy of remuneration by the management.

Thus it comes as no surprise to learn that in the 1986–87 season, while Bryan Robson was on a basic of £98,000 and Jesper Olsen £85,000, Norman, the gilded youth, the man who had done everything for the reds, whose goal had won the Cup two years previously, was on £45,000 a year. Robson, no one would begrudge, but what kind of free market values Jesper Olsen as worth nearly twice as much as Norman Whiteside? And let's not even mention the fact that, ten years later, Andy Cole is making in ten days what Norman made in a year.

'I suppose it does piss you off a little bit when you find out you're not in the A team of earners,' the man himself said, taking the institutionalised mean-spiritedness in his giant stride. 'But I have no grudges. I was earning good money compared to the working-class guy in the street and I was playing for Manchester United. You couldn't ask for anything more.'

No one realised it at the time, but that Cup final in 1985 was probably the apex of his career. True, he was on rampant form the next year as United sprinted through autumn towards the title, but by the spring it had ended in ignominy and, thanks to Liverpool fans behaving badly in Brussels, there was to be no European stage on which to demonstrate his skill and power. Then, in 1986, Norman went to his second World Cup and came back injured. By the time he had fully recovered his fitness, his father figure, Big Ron, was gone.

'I remember I was in the physio room as usual in the Cliff when he called me into his office and said, you know, it's over, and could I call the lads together. They were training over at Littleton Road, and so I went over there and gathered them together; it was me I suppose who broke the news. Then we all went into the gym and Ron came in and told us all. Then he said: "Back to my office for a party." Ron's the only bloke I know who could throw a party the day he was sacked. We all ended up back at his place. It was a Thursday; I think it was one of those Thursday nights when I broke the rules and had a little drink. I remember Ron said, as he poured me a half, your new manager Alex Ferguson will be here tomorrow. And I remember thinking, that'll be interesting. The next morning, Fergie arrived and we all met him down the Cliff and I don't think me and Big Paul [McGrath] were fully concentrating, shall we say.'

Publicly at least Alex Ferguson was a Norman Whiteside fan. He admired his bravery and touch, and he was one of many to make the Kenny Dalglish comparison. But under Fergie, the injuries came ever more frequent and ever more damaging and the manager seemed to lose patience. Norman soon became a bit-part player, turning up occasionally in midfield or attack, renowned less now for his skills than his bite. When he did appear, such as in that game against Liverpool, his legend was only enhanced. We on the terraces continued to love him, continued to see him as the embodiment of all we stood for, our man on the pitch. We chanted his name when he wasn't playing, wrote to *The Manchester Evening News* demanding Fergie picked him, whinged endlessly in pub conversations. But we didn't know what was going on behind the scenes; didn't know how bad those injuries were; didn't know how the Whiteside morale had been knocked by sudden incapacity; didn't know how determined Ferguson was to alter the whole complexion of the club.

In the 1988–89 season, cut down by an achilles and then a knee problem, the Scouse Buster played only six times. And then we began to hear the rumours: Fergie didn't want him; he was going to be transferred; the Italians were interested; Liverpool had offered £1.5 million. We couldn't believe what was happening. He was still only 23, surely a bit of patience and he would be back to greater glory. Time, after all, was on his side. Here was, we felt in those grim, dark early Fergie days, proof of our leader's poor man-management skills. And the end the rumour-mongers had been predicting finally came in August 1989.

'I was in Belfast doing my summer schools, and I got a call from him saying come over,' Norman remembered. 'We'd agreed a date for me to come back and now he wants me early. I thought, aye-aye. I went into his office and he told me he'd been given X million to spend on superstars and I wasn't part of his plans. I found this hard to take, you know; I could see it coming, but talks like that are always hard to take. I'd been there since I was a kid. It was, you know, hard, tears. He said Colin Harvey was interested in me and should he phone him. I said yes.'

He and Ferguson fell out big time, was the story. 'People say I fell out with Fergie, he did this, I did that. Truth is, we got on fine, I never had any trouble with him at all. One thing about Fergie, he's a straight guy. He's a grass-roots person, working-class like us all. He said to me: "Look, Norman, you're going there as a superstar; ask for XYZ." He said: "Here's what you could get, go to Everton and earn a few quid." So I went and I earned more in two years at Everton than I did in my entire United career.' But boy, did we miss him. And Everton, they got a steal: Norman Whiteside for £750,000? It was a joke.

As it generally does, time proved Ferguson right. Hubris, the ancient Greek explanation for the manner in which those who fly too high too soon are doomed to fall, made a big-time appearance in Norman's life. He played 27 league matches for the Toffees and was looking good, refusing to take it easy or to protect his knees by keeping them out of dangerous places, when it happened.

'It was 28 September 1990,' Norman said, the date etched on his memory. 'I went one way, my leg went the other way and I heard it . . . snap, crackle, pop . . . just in the spot where there was weakness. I thought: "Good night nurse."'

Being Norman Whiteside, he tried. But he had checked in to the physio room for the last time. In June 1991, after nine months of specialists and consultations, weeks at a time spent on the treatment table, his doctors finally persuaded him there was no point trying again. He was 26 and finished.

So where do you go? Sportsmen live on a different time-scale from the rest of us. For them, their career is all over at an age when ours are just taking off. For Norman Whiteside, who had everything before he was 21, the sudden realisation that the whole lot had gone five years later must have been terrifying.

'Ask anyone in the country what they want to be,' he said when I asked him how he felt. 'And they tell you: a footballer. Who do they want to play for? Man United. Like to score in the World Cup finals? You bet. I'm fortunate I've done all these things and that I have pleasant things to look back on and show the kids on video.'

Yes, yes, yes. But that was his past, no one could argue with that. The point was, what about his future? Didn't the thought of that occupy his mind a little?

'It was hard to take,' he agreed. 'But there's no point in sitting around looking for sympathy; it doesn't get you anywhere, does it? I thought, what can I do with my life? So I went back to school.'

The casual, thoughtless image of footballers is this: they're thick. But you only have to see Hansen or Lineker on the telly, or speak to Ray Wilkins or read Garry Nelson's book to realise the shallowness of that observation. What footballers are is uneducated. Ryan Giggs is typical. He has been, to all intents and purposes, a full-time professional sportsman since he was 12. The school-room wasn't a big part of his life. More than that, though, the peer pressure the professional footballer faces is rabidly anti-learning. Willie Morgan, for instance, recalls what life was like at United in the '70s.

'We had a great time, all the banter and the lads,' Morgan told me. 'But I sometimes wish I'd taken advantage of some of the opportunities we had, you know, the travel. There was this macho thing in the dressing-room, you mustn't be seen to be a tourist. You must be cool: cameras were a no-no. I remember once we were playing in France, it may have been with Scotland, and the coach driver took this big detour to show us the Eiffel Tower. He parked the coach up and said: "Right, you've got an hour." And we said: "For what?" And he said: "To look at the Eiffel Tower." And me, from the back of the coach, I lift my head up from the round of cards and says, "Whose deal?" It got a big laugh, but you look back and think . . . '

Norman Whiteside, though, was never like that. 'I got a world education as a footballer,' he told me. 'I travelled the world three or four times. To see different cultures was fantastic. I remember going to Peking with Everton, and me and Big Dave Watson – a great lad, Dave – decided to go to Tiananmen Square. So we left the hotel, took a rickshaw, or whatever, and went to see this place that had been in all the papers a couple of months before. It was incredible, just to see it, to be there. And the rest of the lads looked at us like we'd wasted our time: we could have sat round the pool. I thought, what's the point of going to all these places around the world and not seeing any of them? Most of the lads, they flew into the airport, got on the coach, went to play the game, back to the hotel and then flew to Hong Kong. So they've been to China, but have they really been to China?'

With a curiosity like that, Whiteside found no problem with education. He took his GCSEs, then his A-levels, then, inspired in part by the amount of time he had spent in treatment rooms, he registered in a three-year podiatry course at University College Salford, graduating in June 1996. He paid his way through college by spending his evenings on the after-dinner circuit: a man with all those stories and about half the age of the usual speaker, he is in enormous demand.

I went to see him at the college, when he was about to take his finals. I was shown the way to where we were going to meet by a porter who, given half a chance and the earth-moving equipment, would clearly have dug up as souvenirs the very floor tiles Norman walked on. 'He was the best, you know,' the man said conspiratorially as he led the way. 'I'm red through and through, me. Season ticket holder 20 year now. And Norman, what a guy.'

Norman merged effortlessly into the place, in Ben Sherman shirt, jeans and Kickers and white medical coat; an expensive leather briefcase where a Tesco bag would normally be was the only sign that he was once something more than just a student. He was studying in a room full of feet. There were posters of feet, large models of feet, cutaway diagrams of feet. Feet are his career now. And I thought, as I talked to this modest, engaging, heroic man, how appropriate it was that he had chosen podiatry as his new life: giving something back to feet after a career endangering them. Presumably he'll open his first practice in Liverpool.

OOH, AAH, MINE'S A JAR

Paul McGrath. Life began: 13.11.82

There is one other thing about Norman Whiteside I didn't mention earlier: he likes a drink. And there is one other thing about Bryan Robson, too: he's rather partial to a drop. Paul McGrath, Ireland's hero, the Black Pearl of Inchicore, as they called him in the south, the finest defender ever to slip on a green shirt, similarly has an aversion to a dry throat that borders on the pathological. And when the three of them played in the same United team at the same time as others – such as Gordon McQueen and Kevin Moran – who were dedicated disciples of the God Good Time, the landlords of Manchester wore the biggest grin since Bestie packed up and exiled himself in Los Angeles. It was some team Ron Atkinson built in the mid-'80s. Not just on the park, but in the bar too: the first division champion boozers.

Ever since Bestie set the template, spotting footballers out on the town has become a major Mancunian participation sport (these days Lee Sharpe can't even blow his nose in public without the tittle tattling). I remember in my youth, the *frisson* of excitement when we saw Jimmy Nicholl in our local (probably the only time in his career Nicholl ever gave anyone cause for a *frisson*). I remember a girlfriend telling me – her voice catching with the thrill of it – that she'd been chatted up at a party by Lou Macari (she'd have been less excited had she known this made her about as exclusive as a winner in the first round of the *Readers' Digest* numbers draw). I remember another girl I knew telling me she had got very friendly with Joe Jordan in a pub in Sale and that he was really boring. And then seeing her a couple of weeks later and her saying how pissed off she was he hadn't rung. If we got worked up and emotional about that, imagine what it was like in the mid-'80s.

In the mid-'80s, during the Lawson boom, when in the City of London greed became good, in Manchester it was gossip about the off-duty activities of the city's footballers that was the premium commodity. Everyone had a United yarn to tell, and traded it on with interest. There was the one about Robbo at a nightclub being so involved in his pint he walked into the ladies by mistake. There was one about Norman Whiteside side-stepping the dull, suffocating convention of licensing hours and spending several days drinking with Paul McGrath, a short break from reality which culminated in the two of them appearing on Granada's *Kick Off* programme (Tommy Docherty's favourite viewing) looking less than shevelled. And there was the one about Paul McGrath driving home from another extended social engagement, this time with the builders who had just finished work at Norman Whiteside's house (he wasn't fussy). About how he was not, shall we say, fully alert behind the wheel. About how he missed a substantial bend in the road and put his car instead into a hedge. And about how, when the police arrived at the scene and saw the wreckage, they couldn't believe anyone could escape with their life and were just about to file a fatality report when a big black Irishman got out of the car and wished them top of the morning.

Of course we were reluctant to believe any of these wild and ludicrous stories about our red-shirted heroes. Our first instinct was to assume they were professional athletes, tucked up early in their bed with a vitamin drink and an improving book, preserving their energies, letting nothing disturb the equilibrium of the finely-honed machine that was their bodies. But boy, were the stories persistent.

Ron Atkinson, it seems, was an indulgent manager: 'I don't believe in running a football club like a prison camp' was his ethos. As long as the players turned up for training, he wasn't too worried what they got up to during the week; they were adults after all. They knew the rules – not even being seen in the same premises as alcohol up to 48 hours before a match – and he trusted his lads to stick to them. Though, according to Bryan Robson, the Big One was often flexible about even those rules. Unlike most other managers, he would encourage a player to have one or two pints the night before an important game if he thought it would help them sleep.

Now since Ron was so lenient a leader, his charges were free to make up their own minds, decide on their own social codes, explore their own limits. Bryan Robson, for instance, was – typically – thoroughly professional in his drinking, a Captain Marvel of a boozer. The occasional mishap with a balloon proffered by members of Greater Manchester Constabulary notwithstanding, Robbo never got into any scrapes or difficulties while out on the ale. He was never knee-capped in a pub gents', nor did he nut anyone in a nightclub car-park, nor end up in a scrap with a gang of Scousers at Chester Races. The stories about him generally went along the lines of: 'Hey, guess what, I saw Robbo down the pub on a Monday night.' Yeah and what was he doing? 'Er, having a couple of drinks.'

Robson held his responsibility to the good name of the club sacrosanct. True, he used alcohol as an escape, a release from the pressure, but he never seemed to lose control. Which was going some given the amount he could put away: 20 pints in a night, was the awed rumour. But then, as he proved in his playing career, Robson has an extraordinary physiology. His physical make-up meant that he could drink more in a night than many could in a month and still be the quickest in training the next morning. And it means that now at 39 he looks ten years younger. Even close up, the prying eye can detect none of the liverish sags of the serial drinker: the nicks and scars around his eyebrows are more evidence of battle than booze.

Linford Christie, though, has never touched a drop of alcohol. The great runner won't even drink tea or coffee; nothing passes his lips which might detract from his performance. All you have is your body, is his way of thinking, don't mess with it. It makes you think, what might Robson have achieved had he followed the Linford line and never touched something as athletically debilitating as booze?

'If you have a reputation where you like a few pints,' Robbo told me, 'then as soon as you have a bad game then everyone says he must have been out drinking this week. But the reasons people have bad games are not that simple. It's like saying when someone who doesn't drink has a bad game he's been eating too many fish and chips. I just think as long as you drink in moderation and stay well away from games, then it will not affect you because you are fit and training every day and so you'll soon run a few pints off you.'

There are plenty in football who would disagree, however; who think the endemic use of alcohol by British players is restricting the development of the game in this country. No way we'll ever win anything, one prominent manager once told me, the amount we booze.

'I have these players on a Saturday, think they know all about diet and energy foods,' he said. 'They go to the pre-match meal all serious and saying: "I'll just have a banana." I say to them: "What's the point of that?" And they say: "High in nutrients, good digestive qualities, high in iron and gives a burst of energy." And I think, what the bloody hell's the point of one banana on a match day when I know for a fact their body's been swimming in booze all bloody week.'

Up at Middlesbrough, Bryan Robson clearly does not follow that line. Indeed, though he accepts that excessive, constant boozing will affect a player's game, he believes drink has another, more significant, role in the life of the professional footballer, beyond mere relaxation. He reckons it can help in bonding a side together; that it is around the pub table that *esprit de corps* is established.

And so, as United skipper, every time he felt morale was slipping in the side, or when he thought a couple of dressing-room issues needed sorting out, he considered it part of his responsibilities to sort out the problem. If there was no mid-week game, on a Monday afternoon after training the skipper would call a team meeting. And when he did, wives and girlfriends would be alerted that they would not be seeing their man that day. The lads would then repair to a friendly hostelry (generally the Park in Altrincham, run by the sympathetic Pat Crerand) and Robbo would get the first round in. Management was strictly not invited.

'When you've had four or five pints,' Robson said of the meets, 'tongues get loosened. Everybody tells a few home truths, things get sorted out then. And you get to know each other as lads, get to know the strong personalities and mebbes those not too strong.'

All sorts of things were worked through at team meetings – new signings were integrated into the side, young players made to feel part of the set-up – and if there was nothing to work through, just having a good time together would bond. The Italians, of course, don't drink like this. Nor do the Spaniards, or the French, or the Portuguese. The Danes do, however, and the Czechs, and the Germans. And, Robbo would suggest, it is significant that the

Willie Morgan steps out
for the 1970 FA Cup
semi-final, complete with
ball, three-tier coiffure and
his own private marching
band (© Exotica)

Martin Buchan warms
up for his début against
Spurs on 4 March 1972.
In the background
Bobby Charlton seeks
out Willie Morgan –
looking to borrow some
hair (© Exotica)

Gordon Hill, a footballing magician known as Merlin.
He failed, however, to cast much of a spell over Dave Sexton

Bryan Robson, the greatest living Englishman, celebrates the news that, thanks to changes in the licensing laws, Pat Crerand's pub will now be open all day (© Steve Hale)

Norman Whiteside (top) and Paul McGrath (bottom): suggesting that, since they were both Irish, they might like to share lodgings was not Ron Atkinson's shrewdest piece of man-management (© Steve Hale)

Mark Hughes cleans up in the 1988 Biggest Thighs in Britain contest (© Steve Hale)

Ryan Giggs running down the wing. Fearful blues not pictured (© Steve Hale)

Steve Bruce and trophy: it must have got boring lifting them after a while (© Steve Hale)

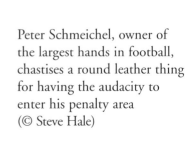

Peter Schmeichel, owner of the largest hands in football, chastises a round leather thing for having the audacity to enter his penalty area (© Steve Hale)

Eric Cantona, Euro star (© Steve Hale)

Alex Ferguson, great Scot (© Steve Hale)

English, the soaks of world football, boast teams that never implode in international tournaments in the manner of the Dutch or the Russians. True, they don't qualify all that often, but when they do, they battle for each other. It is an ethos, he believes, partly shaped in the saloon bar: the team that drinks together, plays together. Indeed, maybe the tabloids got it all wrong and that far from undermining the enterprise, it was a lengthy session in Hong Kong on a pre-tournament tour that invested England with the kind of togetherness that enabled them to play with such spirit in Euro 96. And who was it who inspired that bout of bonkers in Honkers? Bryan Robson.

Drinking, Bryan Robson would thus argue, can have its place. But not all the consumption in Ron Atkinson's lax last days was Robbo-directed team-building. With the boss distracted by what Norman Whiteside calls 'a domestic situation', the boys got into the habit of socialising. And, though Moran, McQueen and Robson were always handy over a pint, the biggest pair of like-minded social souls were Norman Whiteside and Paul McGrath.

'People used to say to us we drank like a pop group: INXS,' Whiteside recalled. 'Robbo, myself, Big Paul, Gordon McQueen and Kevin: we were what you call in golf big hitters, but me and Paul never went near a golf course. We had a great time, no denying we didn't have. I wouldn't change it. No way. Regardless of what people say, I am the one who knows the truth and I'm happy with myself. It just cheeses me off a little bit when people say: "Oh, they drank too much, they drank too much." We only used to drink when it was appropriate. You wouldn't catch us out the night before a game. I only broke the curfew a couple of times in my entire career, and one of those was the night Ron was sacked. We were always first on the team-sheet, we had a little bit of success, so we didn't do too bad.'

He was right: they were great players all. But the problem was, when Alex Ferguson became manager in November 1986, he had a different definition of the word 'appropriate'.

Fergie knew the stories. He had heard that Arnold Muhren, in his autobiography, had said that when he turned up for training first thing in the morning, the dressing-room at the Cliff stank of booze. From the moment the new man arrived, he started receiving the stories first hand from fans rich in that Mancunian currency: gossip. Ferguson believed that there was nothing wrong with a drink – he'd run a pub when he'd first retired from playing, after all – as long as it was in celebration of a job well done. At United, he reckoned, it had become too intimately woven into the fabric of the daily round.

'The main thing is,' the boss wrote of his early days in his book, *Six Years at United*, 'that I didn't want people to get the impression that drinking was part of life at Manchester United.'

Ferguson was appalled by what he found at the club when he arrived. The youth system was undervalued, morale in the reserves and junior teams was very low, and, even worse, first-team preparation had become slack. Never mind a few pints, towards the end under Ron a player wouldn't have run off a half shandy at training. Fergie was also alarmed by the number of injuries, by the constant recourse to the physio's room, by the fact he could rarely pick the team he wanted. It didn't help his opinion that two of the most frequent injury victims were the two most exuberant socialisers: Paul McGrath and Norman Whiteside. Putting two and two together, the bollockings were frequent and severe. After 18 months of sparring, it was during the 1988–89 season that the understanding gap between management and McGrath in particular became unbreachable.

It may seem trite to say it, but a footballer's life is centred around playing the game. The whole enterprise – the training, the tactics, the banter – is geared towards match day. To miss out on that focus, to watch it unfold from the loneliness of the physio room, is to have your very purpose removed. At the beginning of the 1988–89 season, Whiteside retained a serious achilles problem which had not responded to treatment over the summer. McGrath returned from the European Championships in Germany (where he had performed astonishingly when Ireland beat England in Stuttgart) with his knee causing him all sorts of pain. He played the first four league matches, and then the knee went. In October 1988 he had a series of operations, during which the specialist told him he had a career expectancy of three months. Thus the pair had the central pillar of their lives cut away from them simultaneously. The enormous gap where games used to be, they filled by lunching together. Sometimes their lunches would last several days. Ferguson was not amused.

'There was an enormous problem relating to his off-field behaviour,' Fergie wrote of Whiteside. 'I believe most of his problems were down to disappointment and possibly depression with his continual injury. I believe he sought refuge in a lifestyle which, of course, created conflict with my concept of a Manchester United player . . . Paul I was never sure about because you never got any dialogue with him. He just nodded his head, agreed with everything you said, left the room and continued on his merry way. Nothing I said or did seemed to matter to him.'

As the two of them began to recover their fitness, it soon became obvious they had lost the trust and respect of the manager. The bollockings turned to fines, new players were bought to cover the gaps, the future looked non-existent. For McGrath, however, aggressive impositions of discipline were counter-productive: he was a man who needed approbation to function.

'He's right about the drinking binges myself and Norman would go on,' McGrath wrote in his book, *Ooh, Aah, Paul McGrath*. 'We'd be in this pub or that pub and all the time someone would ring Fergie at the club and give him a progress report. I imagine him now sitting at his desk with a map of Greater Manchester, plotting our drinking route. I'm glad he was keeping note of where we were. Usually by the end of the night we wouldn't have a clue and we'd care even less.'

Ferguson and McGrath was not a marriage made in heaven. It wasn't even a marriage of convenience. In January 1989, after McGrath had played a mere three games after a comeback from his injury, it became clear there was only one direction the relationship was heading: the divorce courts. In what might be best described as a misunderstanding, McGrath assumed the recurrence of his knee problem meant he had been stood down by the manager from duty for a cup-tie against QPR. Depressed that he was injured yet again, he went on a bender with the still-side-lined Whiteside, which culminated in a well-refreshed appearance on Granada's *Kick-Off* on the Friday night. Ferguson, however, assumed his player was on stand-by and, with a flu crisis, demanded McGrath make himself available when he turned up to watch the game on Saturday afternoon. McGrath refused, said he was in no fit state to play, that his knee was impossible. At this refusal, that little nerve below Ferguson's eye which twitches when he is anxious went into overdrive.

Banning the entire squad from drinking in public places at any time for the rest of the season was just the start of it. McGrath himself was in for more significant punishment. At a formal and frosty meeting the following week between McGrath, Ferguson, Martin Edwards and club secretary Ken Merrett, the management told him the end of the road had been reached, he was finished and perhaps the best thing, given the medical reports, was to quit the game altogether. A compensation package was offered, which the player turned down: he preferred, he said, to fight his way back into the reckoning. Which he did. He was back in the side a fortnight later, and stayed on to play enormously during the spring of 1989. Characteristically, whatever was going on behind the scenes, Ferguson backed his player publicly: 'McGrath is now right back to his best,' he told a press conference after one game. 'Paul showed today that he is definitely on his way back.'

Privately, though, McGrath believed he was receiving other signals. After he was fined for turning up late yet again for training, the player demanded a transfer. Ferguson refused; his defensive cover was, at the time, too frail to let him go. Word leaked that a transfer had been asked for, and McGrath got booed at his next home match (at Old Trafford, we don't like players who want to leave us). Stung by this reaction, McGrath sought the boss's permission to tell his side of the story to the press. Ferguson refused it. There seemed little hope of a reconciliation. Eventually that summer, when an offer of £450,000 came in from Graham Taylor at Aston Villa, Ferguson decided to let the player go. The manager tracked the player down at Bryan Robson's house, where he was enjoying a summer barbecue, and gave him Taylor's phone number. The pair never spoke again.

While Norman Whiteside took his departure from the club he loved with a good deal of dignity, refusing ever to bad-mouth the manager or even tolerate a word against him, McGrath immediately became engaged in a bitter battle of words the like of which had not been heard since the day Tommy Docherty told Willie Morgan not to come on the club tour. Within a couple of weeks he had sold his story to *The News of the World*. His complaints centred on Ferguson's calvanistic attitudes to relaxation: if he had a drink and lightened up, was McGrath's ghosted analysis, he'd be a better manager. Ferguson was furious and so were the FA. McGrath was landed with a fine of £8,500 for bringing the game into disrepute, the biggest in football history until Vinny Jones was clobbered for fronting a video celebrating the art of the hatchet man. Then Ferguson published a book which, in his efforts to explain to United fans why he let McGrath go, questioned the player's intelligence and suggested he had embarked on an advanced course of self-destruction.

'Popular opinion seems to have it that after he moved to Aston Villa, Graham Taylor found the right way to handle him, giving him a professional minder, more medical help and the like,' Fergie wrote in *Six Years At United*. 'I must tell you, we offered him every facility and advice we could think of. Sir Matt Busby spoke to him along with the club doctor, Francis McHugh; we even got his parish priest in to try and help.'

McGrath tried to stop the book's publication, but was persuaded against it on the grounds of cost. Instead he responded with his own version of events in the book *Ooh, Aah, Paul McGrath*, a prolonged exercise in self-justification, which included the revelation that not only had Ferguson not called in his parish priest to help, but if he had McGrath wouldn't have listened: he had been brought up a Protestant.

So why is Paul McGrath, the big-boozing injury-magnet, the whinger who couldn't get on with one of the best managers in history simply because the bloke told him that bar fly and professional footballer were incompatible occupations, there at the heart of a United Dream Team? He's there because the day I heard that Paul McGrath was on his way I almost wept. And I wasn't the only one. According to Mark Hughes, there were a few raised eyebrows too among the players when he went. We were all unhappy because McGrath was, as he has proved for eight years in Aston Villa and Ireland's colours, the finest defender of his generation. 'The best in the world bar none,' Ron Atkinson called him in 1993. 'Imagine what he'd be like if he had two knees,' Kevin Richardson, his Villa colleague, added.

Alex Ferguson might have chosen not to try, but you don't have to be Anthony Clare to work out Paul McGrath. There are clues right from the start. He was born in Ealing in December 1959. But any thought he might have turned out for England is ill-founded. He is Irish all right, the progeny of a liaison between a young woman from Dublin and a Nigerian medical student. The Ireland of the '50s wasn't the most liberal of places. Such liaisons were not the social norm; his mother fled to England to give birth and immediately she returned to Dublin handed the young Paul over to a Protestant foster home. Try as they might, such places are not renowned for developing self-confidence: Eton they aren't. And when you're the only black kid in town, you tend to be uncertain of your own ability. By 17, the age at which Norman Whiteside had played in the World Cup, the shy, nervous and rejected Paul McGrath was still engaged in park kickarounds. The thing was, he could play in them and eventually someone noticed and he got picked up by a junior team in Dublin. Such were his performances, within a year he had moved on up to a semi-professional side in Dun Laoghaire, which boasted Billy Behan, the eminent Manchester United scout who had discovered Liam Whelan, Johnny Giles and Gerry Daly, as life president. Behan, seeing the calm, quick, commanding lad in action, reckoned he had a find there and tipped off United. Dave Sexton asked to be kept informed.

In the summer of 1979, McGrath went on a tour of Germany with the team, discovered booze and got kicked in the head during a friendly. It may have been the kick, it may have been the sudden realisation he was out alone in the world, it may have been the combination of the two with a few bottles of schnapps to help the brew, but on his return to Ireland he fell into a deep catatonic depression, a black hole, in which he spent the best part of a year sitting on his bed, rocking slightly, silent. A man barely alive, he was finally talked out of it by his football chums who told him, constantly and daily, he could make it as a player. In 1980, a couple of months after he had snapped out of his self-imposed Trappist vows, McGrath signed for St Patrick's Athletic, the senior Dublin side. His first few months were traumatic. Riven with self-doubt, he simply couldn't cope, wondering why he had stuck his head over the parapet, desperate to return to anonymity. His nervy mood wouldn't have been much helped if he had known Behan had cut a deal with United: they would take him if he could prove his mental toughness through a season in the League of Ireland.

Fortunately he was proving too good a player for a few self-doubts to get in his way. Now turned into a centre-back he was adored by the Dublin crowd, who named him the Black Pearl of Inchicore. A Hollywood synopsis of his life would suggest at this point that at last he had found someone to love him. So much was he fancied that in

1982, after Luton, Watford and Manchester City all made offers for him, he was at last invited over by Manchester United for a trial. At his St Pat's leaving party he tried Southern Comfort for the first time. He liked what he tasted.

At Manchester United, he did well. So much so that Ron Atkinson paid £30,000 for him, thus wiping out St Pat's debt at a stroke. Ron wasn't so delighted with his new man's appearance: 'I don't sign centre-backs with ear-rings,' he exclaimed. Ron taking exception to someone else's jewellery? Entertainment, remember, not consistency was his middle name.

Indeed, retrospect suggests Ron hardly dealt with McGrath as cleverly as he might. First he screwed him on his contract, putting him on a three-year deal worth £200 a week ('if you don't like it,' was the gist of the negotiation, 'here's a plane ticket back to Dublin'). And secondly he put him in the same digs as Norman Whiteside.

Paul McGrath made his debut against Spurs at Old Trafford on 13 November 1982. The team that day was: Bailey, Duxbury, Albiston, Moses, McGrath, McQueen, Robson, Muhren, Stapleton, Whiteside, Coppell. The score was 1–0, Arnold Muhren getting the goal, and the crowd was 47,869. The big, quick, powerful centre-back was due to play a long time before that, but in a reserve-team game at the end of the previous season against Sheffield United, an opposing forward's studs had embedded themselves in his knee, precipitating a cartilage operation. You sometimes get the feeling someone is trying to tell you something.

For almost exactly four years, McGrath was a giant for United, commanding in the air, explosive on the ground: Big Paul indeed. It was all there in the 1985 Cup final. Everton had already won the title and the European Cup Winners' Cup; they were looking for a historic treble. And they had the team to do it. It boasted the best midfield in the country and, in Graeme Sharp and Andy Gray, the two hottest strikers. To subdue them you needed all your wits about you. Not to mention all your team-mates. In the 80th minute of the game, however, McGrath put a dire square ball in the vague direction of his central partner, Kevin Moran. Peter Reid, then a dynamic midfield battler rather than an elderly grey-head of a manager, spotted the gaffe and nipped in. Moran, about to earn his soubriquet 'The Late Kevin Moran', slid in somewhat tardily. Reid went into orbit, Moran looked contrite as he waited for his booking, and referee Peter Willis, a good foot taller than anyone else on the pitch, sent him off.

At this point Paul McGrath, alarmed that his mate might take umbrage about a pass apparently intended to put him in the nearest accident and emergency department, started to play like a demon. Indeed, with Frank Stapleton alongside him as a temporary partner, he couldn't afford to slip. Time and again he beat Gray and Sharp in the air. Time and again, judging his interceptions with the kind of split-second precision Moran couldn't earlier muster, he got in front of them on the deck. It was Norman Whiteside's goal, it was Mark Hughes's pass, but more than that it was Paul McGrath's defending that won the Cup for United that day. Even John Motson spotted his performance: 'In the humble opinion of this commentator, Paul McGrath is quite possibly one of the contenders for man of the match.' As Motty equivocated like a Liberal MP, the pictures on the screen showed McGrath, Whiteside and Moran, the team within a team, the unit forged in drink, engaged in a joyful Irish jig on the pitch edge, arms wrapped round each other, yelling ecstatic cheeriness in each other's faces. Paddy Crerand's pub, you couldn't help thinking, was in for quite a night.

Wembley saw McGrath in equally dominant, treble-smashing form nine years later. It was the Coca-Cola Cup final, and this time he was wearing the claret of Aston Villa and it was United chasing history. There was a lot motivating Villa that day: the entire team remembered how they had lost the title to United the previous year; Big Ron, their manager, was keen to put one over on the outfit that had sacked him; and Paul McGrath wanted to show Alex Ferguson that a drink never hurt anyone. Almost qualifying for the veteran's circuit McGrath, by now unable to train because of the suspect nature of his knees yet still capable of winning the PFA Player of the Year, was magnificent as he orchestrated as significant a shut-out as that May afternoon in 1985. He restricted the then-rampant Mark Hughes to one late, pointless goal. Villa won it convincingly, 3–1, and once more he was quite possibly one of the contenders for man of the match.

Even now, seven seasons on, you can't help feeling getting rid of Paul McGrath was one of the few mistakes of Alex Ferguson's decade in charge. Not one that has had a significant effect on his record, clearly. But a mistake nonetheless. Under pressure to succeed, Fergie, the great man-manager, misread the big, quiet Irishman. He mistook diffidence for lack of commitment, a bad patch for a terminal decline; instead of putting an arm round the shoulder, he booted the backside. He would argue he had to change the ethos of the club, whatever the cost to individuals. And that is, naturally, his prerogative. But me, I'd have liked to have seen a place for Paul McGrath in Fergie's dream team.

Luckily for both, there has been rich, rewarding life after divorce: neither can look back with much regret. At the time it was all very different. A shy, insecure man, McGrath hates publicity, loathes the camera, the microphone, the notebook. During the break-up with United in the spring of 1989, which coincided (not much help to anyone) with the break-up of his marriage, he was constantly in the papers. The rumours were epic even by Mancunian standards. In the midst of the crisis, a colleague of mine rang him to offer a sympathetic hearing, an opportunity to present his views in an intelligent interview in a broadsheet paper. McGrath declined; not his scene, he explained, being interviewed; besides, he was approaching the end of his tether.

'All this pressure from all sides,' he said. 'It's enough to turn a fella to drink.'

NOT A GREAT GOAL-SCORER, APPARENTLY

Mark Hughes. Life began: 30.11.83

What you remember, can't get out of your mind, is the noise. A flat, hollow thump, followed, a nano-second later, by a metallic zing. Then an incoherent gargle of a roar, which, you realise within a couple of moments, comes from the lower reaches of your own throat. Then a lot of flailing around and shouting 'yes'. A photo taken then would make you look back and think: what a twat. But at the time you are in a place well beyond the reach of embarrassment; you just jump around with your arms round anyone you can find, exhausting yourself with the pleasure, the relief of it. Then, after a minute or so, you think, thank God I got a ticket for the United section: I wouldn't have been able to keep quiet after that one.

That's what happened when Mark Hughes scored against Oldham in the FA Cup semi-final at Wembley on 10 April 1994. It happened also when Mark Hughes scored the third against Crystal Palace in the FA Cup final at Wembley on 12 May 1990. And – though I was watching in the pub at the time – what happened when Mark Hughes scored the second against Barcelona in the European Cup Winners' Cup final at Rotterdam on 15 May 1991. 'He's taken it too wide,' yelped Brian Moore on the commentary, as Hughes rounded the Barca keeper and blasted the ball goalwards. 'No he hasn't, he's done it.'

A scorer of great goals, not a great goal-scorer: that's the succinct analysis of Mark Hughes as first offered by David Lacey in *The Guardian* in 1988. Not a lynx-eyed Lineker of a tap-in man, but a purveyor of net-busters to send the crowd barking. But in truth

Hughes was always more than that. He was a player not simply capable of contributing incendiary, fabric-threatening efforts to the red cause, but of delivering them at the moment they were most required.

If Eric Cantona is – rightly – credited with winning the 1995–96 double for United, it was, no question, Mark Hughes who won it in 1993–94. Because when United began extra time in that FA Cup semi-final that spring, they looked a team capable of winning nothing – precisely nothing. For six months they had played with flash and panache, with eagerness and rhythm. Now, getting nervy on the final bend, they performed with all the grace and style of Cliff Richard singing in the Centre Court rain. They had just lost the Coca-Cola Cup final and with it the treble to fat Ron and his mighty McGrath; Blackburn had, as if from nowhere, appeared on their shoulder in the league, winning comprehensively a week earlier at Ewood Park; and for 90 minutes the most-limited team in the Premiership had been threatening to boot them out of the Cup. Confidence: the United boys had completely forgotten where they had left it lying around.

Thus when Oldham scored with ten minutes to go, it came as no surprise. Schmeichel, who had been tense and shouty all afternoon, wafted a huge limp mitt at a corner and padded the ball down at the former City player Neil Pointon's feet. He scored, as you knew he would. You watched the Oldham fans jigging their victory jig below you, you imagined how the rest of the nation must have cheered, how the *Schadenfreude* would have flowed in pubs from Newcastle to Penzance (well, the one pub in Penzance that isn't a United pub). When Pointon scored you didn't think it was all over. You knew it was. Shattered after this certain defeat you knew your boys would lose at Leeds in the league the following Wednesday. You knew it. The treble, the double, the single, you knew were all lost in a week.

But Mark Hughes doesn't have the average supporter's predilection for despair. He didn't think it was all over. A man stubbornly keen on diverting history in his own direction, he wasn't going to let it happen. With a couple of minutes of the game left, after the bloke next to me had gone home in head-shaking disappointment, Nicky Butt hoisted the ball forward and Brian McClair chipped it on, over an advancing line of blue and red. It fell, apparently slower than the laws of physics allow, over Mark Hughes's left shoulder and, as he tumbled backwards to develop greater purchase, it dropped towards his right foot. And that was when the noise started, when the social niceties were temporarily and gloriously put to one side.

A tap-in wins you a match, that goal of Hughes's won a season. No exaggeration: its very drama reinvigorated the cause, reinvested it with self-belief, revitalised the effort as if by giant injection. Three days later Oldham were murdered in the Cup replay and so, when the rearranged game was finally played, were Leeds in the league. The double was as good as secured with that goal. And only one man on the pitch could have scored it.

'I just couldn't see a goal coming,' said Joe Royle, then Oldham's manager, after the game. 'It was going to take something out of the blue. When the ball dropped, it would have gone over the stand with most players. But unfortunately for us it fell to Mark Hughes. You can't legislate for that kind of strike.'

Two years almost to the day after he scored that goal, I interviewed Mark Hughes for the *Manchester United Family Tree* television programme. We caught up with him early one morning, before he went off training with Chelsea (at which – you don't score goals like he does by accident – he practises volleying incessantly). His new team's season had just been ended a couple of days earlier when they were beaten in the FA Cup semi-final by United, a game which even Hughes couldn't swing. 'It's the first time in six years I've not been involved in something at the end of a season,' he said, sounding down – well down. 'It's a very strange feeling. I'm not sure why we're bothering.'

When you're addicted to drama, the withdrawal isn't easy.

Yet for a man who seems to precipitate such excitement on it, off the pitch Mark Hughes is a singularly undemonstrative person. Before the match in Barcelona in the Champions League in the autumn of 1994, for instance, Hughes was besieged by the local press who were seeking the views of the one visitor who had played regularly at the Nou Camp. At the airport the press men ignored Ince and Schmeichel, Giggs and Sharpe, as they carried their hand luggage through customs, and folded instead around Hughes. Such had been the demand from the locals, Alex Ferguson asked his centre-forward to sit with him and Steve Bruce at a raised table in the grand ballroom of United's hotel, facing rows of cameras, microphones and notebooks, to host the pre-match press conference. After Ferguson had joked and joshed, and Bruce had delivered his standard platitudes – 'Barcelona are a massive club and you hope for your entire career to be involved in games like this' – attention turned to Hughes. He made very little effort to disguise his expression, a look which suggested he would prefer to be anywhere than in that room at that time (though possibly not out on the Nou Camp pitch, getting a lesson in football, the next evening). The local press were undaunted. With two daily sports papers to fill, they needed quotes and they moved in on him.

What was it like to be back, they wanted to know? Did he have happy memories of their city? Had he been motivated by revenge when he scored against Barca in the European Cup Winners' Cup final three years previously? Did he remember the white handkerchiefs?

After a moment I thought, from my position about ten rows from the front, that he was refusing to answer. And then I realised, as the Catalans moved closer towards the table where he was sitting, straining to hear, that he was talking. It was just that he had a voice which, despite the amplification, could barely project past the third row. 'Sorry, can you speak up,' an English hack yelled from row seven.

Somehow it comes as a real shock to discover that a man with calf muscles apparently crafted from steel, should have the vocal chords of a lost child: soft, modest, nervous. It's not that you expect him to be jerking about like Gazza, but the robustness of his frame and the stamping, snarling passion of his playing, you assume, will be reflected in his personality. Hughes's shyness, though, has played almost as significant a part in his life as those calves. It was, after all, that which got him to Barcelona in the first place.

A bustling midfielder from Ruabon in North Wales, Mark Hughes had been receiving Christmas cards from United, with solicitous messages about the future being red, since he was 12. If they wanted him that badly, he thought, why be churlish, and he joined the club as a 14-year-old schoolboy, personally signed up by Dave Sexton. 'I'd been there a few months when I realised I'd not heard him speak,' said Hughes – quietly – of the man who brought him to Old Trafford. 'I thought, this is a bit odd, he's meant to be the manager and he's shyer than me.'

After a couple of years as a homesick young apprentice, he appeared to be heading in the direction most junior pros take – the local job centre – when United's youth coach, Syd Owen, switched him to play centre-forward. It was a shrewd move: the skill, strength and mobility of a midfielder allied immediately with the selfish, predatory instincts of the striker which were lurking somewhere in the boy's diffident psyche. In 1982, Hughes played in the Youth Cup final, in a forward partnership with Norman Whiteside. Imagine that, 18 years old and playing centre-back against a pair like that, all hairy and muscular and old before their time. Pants must have been filled across England.

Hughes's goals and line-leading abilities eventually led Ron Atkinson, by now installed in the manager's office, to notice him. Atkinson invited him along on a League Cup jaunt to his old club Oxford United's Manor Ground on 30 November 1983. When Arthur Graham was incapacitated ('He had the trots, I think,' Hughes recalled) just before the game, Hughes was put into the starting line-up out on the left wing. The team that day was: Bailey, Duxbury, Albiston, Wilkins, Moran, McQueen, Robson, Moses, Stapleton, Whiteside, Hughes; the crowd 13,379 and Hughes scored the only goal with a header. He looked less than chuffed at scoring, which might have had something to do with having his big mop of tousled curls ruffled in patronising appreciation by Gordon McQueen. It wasn't just Hughes's goal that caught the eye that day. It was his legs. In the style of the time his micro-shorts were hitched up higher than Sally Gunnell's running knickers, and revealed acres of glistening, muscular thigh, the pistons that drove him hard and fast. They were simply the most powerful legs you have ever seen.

By the end of the season, by now alternating with Whiteside as Frank Stapleton's striking partner, he had scored four goals in seven starts. By the start of the next year, with Whiteside pushed back into midfield, Stapleton injured and Alan Brazil proving a waste of space, Hughes was first-choice forward. As United won the Cup, he scored 24 goals in the season and was voted PFA Young Player of the Year.

Ron Atkinson, though, wasn't convinced. He never really trusted the new Welsh recruit, mistaking his quietness for a lack of interest and driving him further into his shell with relentless mickey-taking. The nickname Sparky was Ron's, incidentally, and its initial purpose was ironic: off the pitch, he reckoned the boy hardly a live-wire personality.

'I'm grateful to Mr Atkinson for giving me my chance,' Hughes said to me when it was suggested the two didn't get on. At which point I thought: Mr Atkinson? Not Ron, not Big Ron, not even the boss, but Mr Atkinson. Here's a millionaire superstar, admired by his peers, worshipped beyond the point of sycophancy by fans, still adopting the respectful language of the schoolboy to describe a manager he hasn't worked with for 12 years. Not exactly pushy, then.

'The point was I was never in his little circle. Mr Atkinson liked to get close to Gordon Strachan, Bryan Robson, forceful characters he liked. I think he had difficulty integrating me into that circle. I was always a very quiet lad.'

Stubborn as well. If Ron didn't take to him, there was no way he was going to ingratiate himself. So there he was, 21 years old, hotter than tabasco and the manager wasn't impressed. He was a manager, too, who got a kick out of driving a hard bargain wage-wise: in 1985 the Young Player of the Year was earning £200 a week. Thanks to Ron's parsimonious reputation, several agents, the new breed of parasite beginning to feed off the body of football, sensed they could get a deal here. Thanks to Hughes's shyness, he couldn't tell any of them to get lost.

'I had four or five agents I was involved with at the time,' he recalled. 'And they all advised me not to sign my new contract when it was offered. When word got out that I hadn't signed, there was a lot of interest in me, which was very flattering. Instead of nipping the speculation in the bud, I let it go on. I had Italian waiters coming up to me in restaurants saying they represented this and that; it was getting ridiculous in the end.'

It got even more ridiculous when Hughes began the 1985–86 season like he wanted to win the league on his own, by Christmas. He was enormous that autumn. He had developed into the complete centre-forward, leading the line, holding the ball up until reinforcements arrived, pulling the defence out of position, working, working, working. Scoring goals, too. In the 15-match unbeaten start to that league season he bagged ten: not just a scorer of great goals, but a great goal-scorer. And then Terry Venables, the best judge of a player this side of Alex Ferguson and at the time manager of Barcelona, made an approach.

When Ron Atkinson picked up the phone to Terry Venables in September 1985, it was a mistake that, ultimately, cost him his job. El Tel offered £1.8 million to take the young bull to Spain and Ron accepted. Ron figured that Hughes wanted to leave the club anyway – he hadn't signed his contract after all. Besides, he didn't really have much time for the lad and he could use what was then an awful lot of money to buy a few he fancied. His chairman didn't object to the deal: Martin Edwards had a clause in his contract giving him a percentage of outward transfers and a slice of £1.8 million would come in handy supporting a lifestyle renowned throughout Manchester. And so the two of them sanctioned the sale of the player who was leading them to the club's first championship for 19 years without making any effort to get to understand the lad, or discover what was going on behind that quiet exterior. Sod the league title, at the sniff of pesetas their eyes chinged up like cartoon cash registers.

'United got the wrong message really,' Hughes said, understating wildly. 'They thought I was going anyway. There was a lack of communication. I think if I'd gone in and said: "I don't want to go, I'm having these approaches, can we sort it out?" I would have stayed. But that never happened and things just snowballed and before I knew it I was on a plane.'

So no one at United talked to him about the transfer, let alone tried to talk him out of it? 'I was never close to anyone inside, really. Perhaps if I'd been a bit more open with the senior players and asked for advice I'd have made a different decision. You have to look at it from their point of view. It was an awful lot of money for a player who'd only had one good season in senior football.'

Was it simply a money decision for him too? 'I think if they'd put me on a par with some of the senior players at the time I wouldn't have gone anywhere. But they didn't and I did.'

His advisers, of course, the four or five of them hovering around hoping for sardines to be thrown in the sea, were hardly going to suggest he turn down Barca's offer and thus deprive themselves of some tidy commission. And so a whole, unnecessary, fatuous and farcical train of events was set in place. After an initial approach was made, Hughes, still out of contract, was dithering: at heart what he wanted was a rise and to stay at home. But Ron helped concentrate his mind by trying to encourage him to sign his contract (if he didn't, you see, then he could have gone to Spain as a free agent and United wouldn't have got the fee). Such urgency hardly made the player feel the club were trying to keep him. Thus in January 1986, he decided to go and signed for the biggest club in the world on as neutral ground as you could find: Switzerland.

'I met up with this senior vice-president out in Geneva, signed the contract and then he said we should go and celebrate in this posh restaurant,' Hughes told me. 'I didn't have a jacket and they made me wear this big leather coat at the table. I looked ridiculous. He said: "Why are you looking so glum, it should be the happiest day of your life?" but I just felt so embarrassed. I'm not quite sure what he thought he was dealing with, but he didn't change his mind.'

The leather coat was symbolic: the entire episode was ludicrous. And yet there was one other snag to come. Barcelona already had the maximum number of foreign players allowed by the Spanish FA on their books (Gary Lineker, Steve Archibald and Bernd Schuster, since you ask). They couldn't import another foreigner until the close season, and they didn't want word getting back to these three that someone else was being bought, in case it demotivated them. Hughes was, therefore, asked to keep mum. So he returned to United, where he was expected to lead their attack towards the title, with the burden of a Catalan state secret on his shoulders. He wasn't a comfortable boy.

'I was sworn to secrecy, but the press got wind of it and every day I was asked if I was going or not,' he remembered. 'I had to keep on denying it and the more I denied it, the more I knew I was not being truthful with myself or anybody else and in the end it started to affect me. I'm afraid I'm not the kind of player who can cope with that kind of pressure.'

He took refuge back home in Ruabon as often as he could, preferring, typically, to eschew the first division drinkers around him and turn instead into what he called in his autobiography 'a one-man beer festival'. 'It wasn't quite as bad as that,' he said, looking rather sheepish. 'The publishers told me you have to come up with a line to sell a book, and that was a good one.' Beer festival or not, his form slumped, he stopped scoring and – this was no coincidence – he sat in the middle of the cart as the wheels fell off and United stuttered in fourth in a championship race they had threatened to canter.

That summer he went to Barcelona. He started well enough – in a pre-season friendly against Milan, Ray Wilkins remembers, he played a blinder. But it soon degenerated. Young, shy and stubborn, he lived on toast, alone in a villa, refusing all efforts to integrate, embarrassed even to take up Gary Lineker's frequent invitations to dinner. Within three months, while the ambitious Lineker was making hay and scoring goals, the introverted Hughes was getting miserable and found the greatest opportunity of any footballer's life one he would rather not have. The Catalan fans were not slow to express their impatience with the desperate, muscular, over-aggressive style he adopted in an attempt to play his way out of depression, and waved in his direction the traditional local sign of disapproval when matadors lose their bottle: the white handkerchief.

'It was horrible,' he recalled. 'I remember looking up at the stadium and everywhere you looked you just saw white. But it was my fault. I was out of my depth, a mixed-up lonely Welsh boy who didn't want to be there in the first place.'

Meanwhile in England, Ron Atkinson, losing the plot after United's failure the previous year, a failure he had precipitated by selling Hughes, had been replaced by Alex Ferguson. Fergie wanted Hughes back and made his interest known via the several channels that represented the player. Hughes, by now dropped by Barca, met the new boss on a trip home and was immediately won over by his insistence that, had he been United manager, he would never have sold him in the first place. When you've had 100,000 Catalans waving hankies at you, it's nice to be wanted. After he'd spent the rest of the financial year on loan at Bayern Munich enjoying a tax holiday, United bought him back for £1.6 million. £200,000 profit in just under two years: not a bad bit of flesh trading, until you remember that a league title had been squandered in the rush to achieve it.

If Hughes was pleased to be back, it was nothing compared to the delight on the terraces. We never blamed him for going; our wrath was reserved for the board for selling him, a board who had yet to appreciate that the best way of making money out of a football club is not to asset-strip, but to invest in a team which wins things. The warning cry of 'Youzeh, Youzeh' echoed round Old Trafford as his square-jawed, scowling, aggressive presence made itself felt on opposition defences. You want someone like that in your team, someone who frightens them. And you could tell how effective

Hughes was by how much the fans of other clubs loathed him. I remember sitting behind some Spurs fans when Hughes scored the winner at White Hart Lane once. 'I hate them,' one said, 'but I hate him most of all.' And I remember what happened at Bramhall Lane when Hughes, after scoring a wonder goal, exchanging passes with Ince on the edge of the box and then burying a left-foot shot from 20 yards, was sent off for kicking his marker up the backside. As he walked towards the tunnel to the dressing-room, which was sited directly below where I was sitting, a Sheffield United supporter started haranguing him.

'Oi, Hughes,' she shouted, and he looked up at her. 'Yeah, you. You think you're clever, don't you? Well let me tell you something: you're not.' And then she turned to her companion and said: 'I think I made myself perfectly clear.'

'Aye,' he said. 'You did that.'

His peers, though, they knew what he was. In 1989 and 1991 he was voted PFA Player of the Year. Which wasn't bad, because at the time the pundits said he was impossible to play alongside.

This story came about because the year before he arrived back at the club Brian McClair scored 24 league goals as United came in runners-up. The belief was – not least on the red terraces – that the two of them would develop into the dream pairing which would land the title at last. In their first year together, however, they managed only 24 between them. McClair wasn't blamed – his altruistic running remained intact. Hughes, however, was: for being too selfish and for looking for the stunner when a pass for a McClair tap-in would have been the better option. The player himself, not surprisingly, has another explanation for the dream ticket not quite working.

'Brian did well in his first season, but then Gordon [Strachan] and Jesper [Olsen] left the club and he didn't get the supply he'd had before. Also I think Peter Davenport, who'd been operating on the left, had been good for him and he left. All this coincided with me arriving so the label that I was difficult to play with stuck.'

It is a reasonable reading: you aren't going to get many chances to convert if the man you're looking to for supply is Ralph Milne.

Nevertheless, the pair's early failure in front of goal (McClair in particular was so famished you began to suspect hunger strike) was one of the reasons United were in crisis at the back end of 1989. Eight games without a win, and with only one Hughes goal between them, plus an injury crisis of plague-like proportions, led Alex Ferguson to try Mark Robins out up front for the FA Cup tie against Forest on 7 January 1990. It is widely reckoned that Robins's goal that day saved Alex Ferguson and put United on course for their trophy kleptomania in the '90s. What's often forgotten is that Mark Hughes, the selfish loner who couldn't forge partnerships, laid on Robins's goal with a gorgeous, astute pass caressed by the outside of his right foot. And Hughes, too, did more than his fair share in the final that year, nullifying Ian Wright's brilliant brace for Crystal Palace with two of his own, the second arriving, with typically Hughesian drama, seven minutes from the end of extra-time.

The next season, with Lee Sharpe providing tempting crosses, McClair and Hughes found themselves conquering Europe in the Cup Winners' Cup. It was somehow typical of their relationship that McClair scored the goals which got United to the final, and Hughes bagged the ones which won it. And won it against Barcelona, which must have given him an extra *frisson* of enjoyment.

'No,' he told me, '1991 was not about revenge. I had a chance, a good chance, at Barcelona and I just wasn't up to taking it. I just wanted to show everyone there what I was capable of, because I felt I'd never done myself justice over there.'

And what he was capable of, as thousands of soaked reds at Rotterdam that night will attest, was scoring goals that matter. His second that night was a belter, an individual goal of power, a goal celebrated with one finger pointing crowdwards and his mouth opened in a huge, triumphant, cathartic roar. Which, presumably, nobody heard.

Hughes enjoyed his best times with United, however, when Eric Cantona arrived at Old Trafford. 'They'll never work together' was the considered response of many a press observer on hearing of Cantona's signing but, whether by design or luck, they gelled from the off. Cantona held just behind Hughes, allowing him room to wander; he put balls where Hughes wanted them – to feet; he threaded passes through defences for him and watched them being converted. The Welshman, not a great one for verbal communication, found the foreigner was exactly on his football wavelength.

'I know that the Frenchman has changed my footballing life,' Hughes told David Meek in his book, *Hughesie,* and he celebrated the fact by scoring 26 goals in their first full season together, one, against Sheffield Wednesday in the midst of a 5–0 slaughter, probably the best he has ever recorded. A photograph of Hughes in the process of scoring that goal shows that he hit the ball with such power, at the moment of impact his knee was bent upwards at a ligament-threatening angle of 45 degrees.

Nevertheless, that season which ended in double-winning joy was not one of unalloyed pleasure for Sparky. In the European Cup game in Istanbul against Galatasaray, for instance, when United needed to score to qualify for the next round, Hughes was dropped. It was a decision brought about by the UEFA rules on foreigners, and Alex Ferguson had clearly thought hard about his options, toyed with them mentally for hours, about how Bryan Robson wasn't entirely fit so he needed Roy Keane as cover in midfield, about how Denis Irwin had been dropped from the previous game and it had been a mistake. So Hughes went.

It seemed to me at the time a big mistake. I thought it self-evident that, whatever the ludicrous complications of the UEFA ruling, what you do when selecting a team is first pick the players who would make a difference. Clearly, by his fuming body language, eyes narrowed, jaw set, stomping to the bench behind Alex Ferguson, apparently wearing the same leather coat he'd had when he signed for Barcelona, Hughes agreed. What followed is hardly likely to have changed his mind. When the team plane got back to Manchester early the next morning, knocked out and humiliated, Alex Ferguson was one of the first out through customs. As well as three camera crews, a lone supporter in an anorak had stayed up to greet his return.

'It's your fault, Alex,' the youth yelled at the manager. 'You blew it. You should've played Sparky. He'd have won it for us. It's your fault we're out, you blew it. And you know it.' The look on Ferguson's face suggested he didn't entirely disagree.

'I took it hard,' Hughes told me. 'But Mr Ferguson, he was quite prepared to make those decisions and he stood or fell by them.' So what happened when such a decision was made? Did Hughes keep quiet about it and sulk afterwards as was his habit in the past? 'No, I'd learnt. We'd have a discussion about it.' And how did the debate between the stubborn, taciturn Welshman and the stubborn, noisy Scot go? 'He'd take me to one side and say: "I'm leaving you out." And I'd say: "I don't think you're right." And he'd say: "I hope I am."'

And that was it? That was all that was said? To which the answer was an ironic, knowing smile. And if he said anything, it was even quieter than usual.

All great things come to an end, even Mark Hughes's ten-year association with Manchester United. Typically, though, there was drama involved at the last. When Alex Ferguson signed Andy Cole from Newcastle in January 1995, the portents, not to mention the permutations, looked ominous for Hughesie, by then 31. His hair may resemble a judge's wig, but his pride didn't equip him for life on the bench. Alex Ferguson knew his mind: Cole was young and hot and, so it seemed at the time, the man to convert Cantona's passes. He would be first choice and, though he'd love Hughes to stay, if it was a guarantee of first-team action he wanted, then one couldn't be provided.

Hughes played in what was widely reckoned his last game for United before disappearing westwards for a lucrative couple of years with Everton, at St James's Park on 15 January 1995. But in scoring – naturally – an extraordinary goal, he injured himself. Everton would have to wait. And then Eric Cantona went walkabout on a south London yob's chest, was banned for six months and Hughes suddenly became indispensable. Or at least he was until the final league game of the season when a win at West Ham would have secured the title and the man who could make a difference was dropped and sat on the bench, watching the ball not quite land right for his successor.

It wasn't that alone which decided him. But when, over the summer, Glenn Hoddle called at his baronial home in the Cheshire countryside bearing a large cheque, the player who is partial to a touch of remuneration decided to play out his last couple of years at Chelsea. You could understand his reasoning, you could understand Alex Ferguson's decision to let him go, but to see him trot out at Old Trafford wearing a blue shirt, it hurt. The reception he received when he returned home with Chelsea was enormous: the stands reverberated to the cry of 'Youzeh, Youzeh', a chant given an extra edge of poignancy by Cole's growing inability to replace him adequately. And when Dennis Wise equalised for Chelsea he didn't celebrate. 'I'm not one for making a big song and dance about a goal,' he told me. 'But after the reception I'd got from the United fans it wasn't really appropriate to get all excited about a goal against them.'

Instead he just trotted, head down, quietly, back to the centre circle. Typical Mark Hughes, a man alone amid all the drama breaking around him.

CAPTAIN RESPONSIBLE

Steve Bruce. Life began: 19.12.87

It is always a laugh when a referee gets injured. One in the eye for authority, or, in the case of Michael Peck, one in the calf muscle. When he went down during the match against Sheffield Wednesday on 10 April 1993, Old Trafford rocked with tittering. Not that I was there. I had been to Norwich the previous week with my mate, Nigel, when United had destroyed their championship rivals 3–1 in a display of such corruscating counter-attack that the Canaries fan behind us had given up telling us to sit down and by the end was congratulating us on supporting the best team he'd seen at Carrow Road not just that year, but ever. So I thought, as the Wednesday game was on Easter Monday, I could perform some familial duties confident that the first league title in 26 years was heading our way. And I could catch up with the party on the Wednesday night at Coventry.

Thus I came to be in a gift shop in Stamford, Lincolnshire, plugged in to a Walkman tuned to Radio Five when news came through of Mr Peck's discomfort: the sniggers were transmitted loud and clear. Alan Green appeared to find it as amusing as the crowd, though his excitement at that was nothing compared to the moment when the linesman, who had taken over refereeing duties when it was obvious the man in green couldn't continue, gave Wednesday a penalty within a minute of assuming responsibilities. John Sheridan, the United fan whose free kick had beaten us in the 1991 League Cup final, wasn't going to miss this one either.

Even disengaged, kept in touch with the action via a radio link, there was a horrible sense of an inaction replay the moment the tinny cry of a few hundred opposition fans confirmed Sheridan's goal. The year before, Easter Monday had been the start of the championship nadir, when United had lost at home to Forest, when the title was lost through nerves, when it had been handed to Leeds. So it was happening again: the jitters were back. Ten days after playing like Gods at Norwich, the same team were displaying all the poise and conviction of Dale Winton. I kicked a stuffed Garfield the Cat, which was standing by the shop entrance.

I'd given up and was about to switch off the radio when, from a Dennis Irwin corner in the second minute of time added on for Mr Peck, Steve Bruce nodded an equaliser. Instead of celebrating, Bruce picked the ball out of the net and ran with it to the centre spot: there was more work to be done. Five minutes later, seven minutes after the game should have finished, marooned up in their penalty area, Bruce met a cross from Gary Pallister with his head and scored the winner. Then he celebrated.

Watching *Match of the Day* that night, you could see what his second meant to United. Brian Kidd ran from the dug-out and knelt on the pitch, pounding the turf with his fists and thanking God who – to give us seven minutes of injury-time in which to secure a vital win – he clearly believed to be a red. Kidd was at the ground, and seized by the atmosphere he was temporarily maddened by proximity to the event. When I took up much the same posture as him in the middle of a Lincolnshire gift shop, it was less easily explicable.

For the next few days, the papers were full of whinging Villa and City and Leeds and Liverpool fans citing the seven minutes' injury-time as evidence of an FA–media conspiracy to gift United the championship for commercial reasons. In fact, it turned out that ten minutes should have been added on. But as United fans, we didn't mind. After 26 years, it didn't matter how the championship was won, in the first or the last minute, as long as it was. Those three points against Wednesday, fortuitously gained in Mr Peck's discomfort though they may have been, virtually sealed it.

It was typical that Steve Bruce should score those goals. Not simply because he has some record for a centre-back: he is the highest-scoring defender in post-war league football and his 19 goals in the 1990–91 season is said to be an all-time record for a defender. But because for Steve Bruce no cause is lost. In his philosophy, the game may be deep into injury-time, but you still sling your 12st 10lbs after the ball whatever the time. You don't break your nose four times in the cause, and end up with it smeared over your cheekbones like plasticine, by letting the opposition walk all over you. Who cares if you've not got the speed or the skill; if you've got the heart and the guts, those internal things that drive you, you can do it. That's always been the way with Steve Bruce: if you want it enough, you can get it.

'When he passes on I want his body for medical research,' Alex Ferguson has said of him. 'He's unbelievable. It's hard to know what this man is made of.'

There's a photo in his autobiography, *Heading for Victory*, of Steve Bruce in his school team, the Under-11's at Walker Gate Primary in Newcastle. It shows a bunch of young lads, all much the same in vicar's collared shirts and plimsolls, holding up the local area knock-out trophy – The Bagnall Cup – in 1970. If you were asked to pick out which of those boys was going to succeed, you wouldn't pick Bruce. Although he's in the middle, holding the cup, he doesn't stand out. Not as much as the athletic-looking boy with the confident smile to his right, or the cocky kid on his left, with the mop-top hair flopping in his eyes, head tilted to one side, arms folded and mouth worked into a smirk. Bruce, with the toothy grin and the wobbly hair, just looks pleased to be there.

Making it as a professional footballer, though, is not so much to do with how good you are, even less how good you look; it is to do with your mental strength and your ability to seize opportunity when it arises. School contemporaries of professionals often remember them as no better than the rest. A good player, yes, but not one you thought – wow. But skill isn't everything: indeed, the very fact a player makes it proves he is good enough. The process of becoming a footballer, which may appear to an outsider old-fashioned to the point of inhumane, is designed to provide the knocks and disappointments, the humiliations and scars, the mopping of lavs and the cleaning of boots which will sort the strong from the weak, the committed from the dilettante. If you're the sort to give up at the first instruction to remove that skid-mark from the porcelain, then you'll probably be the sort who will give up when your team's 1–0 down with three minutes of injury-time gone. And Steve Bruce never gave up on his dream of becoming a player. However many bogs he had to clean in the process.

Michael Bell, the teacher in that photo of the Bagnall Cup winners, wrote a note soon after the Cup was won to Mrs Bruce, who appears to have been as willing as her son. 'Thanks a lot for washing the green strip,' he wrote. 'You shouldn't have gone to so much bother. When Steve's playing for Manchester United I don't think you'll have the bother of washing his strip.'

It was just a nice thing to write, Mr Bell thought at the time. Though young Steve wasn't a bad player, he knew the chances of him trotting out in the footsteps of Law, Best and Charlton were roughly on a par with finding the new Elton John in the school orchestra. Certainly the five clubs who turned Bruce down as a trialist, happy to see him because he came from the Wallsend Boys Club production line (that also produced Peter Beardsley and Alan Shearer), didn't believe there was much chance. He traipsed round Newcastle, Sunderland, Derby, Sheffield Wednesday, Bolton and Southport and they all rejected him: a too-small midfielder, high on effort, low on achievement, was their conclusion. He didn't give up, though; even after he'd taken up an apprenticeship at Swan Hunter's shipyard, he carried on with Wallsend. Then at one tournament the team entered in 1977, he was spotted by a scout from Gillingham, who invited him for a trial. Not exactly a hotbed of football, stuck out on the Medway and about as far from home as it is possible to be in the football league, Gillingham nevertheless offered an opportunity, and Steve Bruce wasn't going to let one of them pass. He went down for a week, proved he had the attitude and was offered terms soon afterwards.

After a late-development growth spurt, in the youth team Bruce was converted to a centre-back and made his way through the Gillingham ranks, battling and bustling. He spent six years at the club, got capped by the England youth team and the Under-21s and was loved by the fans who voted him Player of the Year three times. He was also improving his game with every season: by now he wasn't just heart and sinew, he was reading the game with real literacy, getting ahead of forwards by anticipation as much as speed and growing ever more dominant in the air. It came as no surprise when, in 1984, he went up a league or two. Norwich picked him up for a handy £135,000 and he was in the side which won the Milk Cup in 1985 and promotion in 1986. It was a tasty outfit which included Chris Woods, Dave Watson, John Deehan and Mike Phelan and was, in typical small-club style, broken up and sold at the earliest opportunity.

When Alex Ferguson arrived at Old Trafford in the autumn of 1986, he soon found that his centre-backs, skilled internationals though they might be, were constantly injured. McGrath, Moran, Hogg, the unfortunate ME victim Billy Garton: it was hardly the most robust core to his squad. What he wanted was a defence he could rely on and build round, and he realised after the first few months that he would have to buy them in. He had an idea for a back line and started to make inquiries. He wanted Stuart Pearce, but Forest weren't selling; he was luckier with Viv Anderson, but when he was bought from Arsenal, he proved as injury prone as the existing incumbents. With Steve Bruce, though, he hit the jackpot. When he made inquiries about him, Norwich's recently departed manager, Kenny Brown, informed Ferguson: 'You'll love the boy.' Ferguson paid £825,000 for him which, in the annals of Manchester United transfer fees, counts as a snip. It ended at Carrow Road with less dignity than the ever-loyal retainer probably wanted. During a couple of weeks to-ing and fro-ing, haggling and dealing, Bruce, anxious not to get injured, refused to play in a league fixture for the club. Here, after all, was the opportunity of a lifetime presenting itself at United, and he wasn't going to let it go. His replacement in the match suffered an injury which terminated his career.

Thus a chastened Steve Bruce arrived at Old Trafford. He made his debut away at Portsmouth on 19 December 1987. The team that day was: Turner, Duxbury, Gibson, Bruce, Moran, Moses, Robson, Strachan, McClair, Whiteside, Olsen (Davenport). The score was 2–1, Robson and McClair got the goals, the crowd was 22,207 and Bruce broke his nose and gave away a penalty. He was also party to a collective bollocking, Alex Ferguson in crockery-threatening form despite a decent away win. Welcome, Bruce thought, to the land of higher expectations.

Over the next nine years, Steve Bruce epitomised Ferguson's United. No more were they a team with a soft centre, the team left in the box when the title was being handed round. Giggs, Cantona, Hughes, Kanchelskis, they all added the gloss, but the foundations were built round Steve Bruce. Seizing his opportunity, Bruce got better and better at United. With Gary Pallister, he formed a partnership of cement-like consistency. Potential replacements – Donaghy, Parker, May – came, but he stuck at it.

No responsibility was too big for him to take on. In the spring of 1988 Brian McClair gave up taking the penalties after he missed one at Highbury. You couldn't blame him, incidentally. It wasn't so much the miss I remember from that game, it was the verbal haranguing he was subjected to by Nigel Winterburn as he trotted back to the centre circle that probably finished his confidence. Bruce stepped forward, took over and scored spot-kick after spot-kick. In 1990–91, thanks in part to penalties, he scored an incredible 19 goals; it would have been 20 if Mark Hughes hadn't nipped in and made sure his goal-bound header went in against Barcelona in the European Cup Winners' Cup final. And it wasn't just penalties he was prepared to take on board. He also felt responsible for the games of everyone around him, bawling, chivvying, a picture of anguish and outrage at colleagues' every mistake. 'He's like an old housewife on the pitch,' Gary Pallister once said. 'He's always ready to have a shout at somebody.'

Particularly Peter Schmeichel. Their rows became a feature of United, the two of them screaming abuse in each other's faces after every opposition attack. My favourite Bruce–Schmeichel interface was in the FA Cup quarter-final against Charlton Athletic at Old Trafford. With United not on song, and Charlton motoring, a through ball was threaded to Kim Grant, their pacey young forward. It caught Bruce and his chums completely square, statuesque even. Schmeichel, sensing danger, but not aware Paul Parker was covering rapidly, tore out of his goal and proceeded to slide in on the Charlton forward, feet up, as if he was modelling a new range of studs and wanted those on the back row of the main stand to get a good look. As Grant span comically through the Mancunian sky, Schmeichel, just in case the referee hadn't seen the foul, handled the ball. The ref had seen both offences, and sent the keeper bathwards without a second thought. As Schmeichel remonstrated, Steve Bruce arrived, marginally late, on the scene, presumably, you thought, to intercede on his colleague's behalf. Well, not quite; even from high up in the stands with no formal lip-reading skills, there was no question what Bruce said to his beleaguered mate: 'What the fuck are you doing?'

Seizing his chance, Steve Bruce proved a natural leader. Not just on the field, but off it too, helping new arrivals, good with the young players, hosting social gatherings to build team morale.

'As a skipper if they need a little bit of advice or I can point them in the right direction now and again I'll do it,' he has said. And Gary Neville, who appears to be taking Bruce as a head-boy role model, said recently: 'He is the kind of person you strive to be. Everybody likes him. Everybody would go to him and ask him for advice, whether it was a personal or a football problem.'

So when Bryan Robson was injured, he was the one to fill in – notably lifting the Rumbelows Cup in 1992 when he was distraught to be confronted not by a royal handing out the gongs, but the winner of an internal Rumbelows sales incentive scheme. Eventually, when Robson was reckoned beyond it, he took over. His seizure of the arm-band coincided with United's annexation of the league. Typically, though, he insisted that Robson lifted the Premiership trophy with him in 1993. And then, when Eric Cantona tried to reciprocate by getting Bruce, even though he wasn't playing, to come up and take the FA Cup in 1996, he refused. 'I've had my turn,' he said. 'It's yours now.'

Everyone who looked could hardly fail to notice that Steve Bruce was a top man. Except, apparently, England managers. 'He's the best centre-back I have ever seen,' says Willie Morgan. 'I really rate him. He's the business; the reason, for me, United have done it over the past few years. How he's never been picked for England is one of the great mysteries.'

Not really. Graham Taylor was the manager in his peak years.

There's another way, too, Steve Bruce epitomises the modern United. He's a friendly guy, jolly with the media; he's the one on trips you can laugh with, who'll talk to you. But when you look back on the interviews, try to pick out the juice, it all fluffs away like candyfloss, slipping through your fingers. Here are a few quotes I've elicited from him:

'Old Trafford has often been described as the Theatre of Dreams and, for me, every time I step out on to the pitch it is a dream come true.'

'It takes a while to grasp the size and ambition of the club.'

'When I came here I found myself winning the FA Cup, the European Cup Winners' Cup and United's first League title in 26 years and then doing the double twice as captain. I would never have dreamed it could happen to someone like me.'

Hot stuff, eh? Oddly, we know more about him than most players. We know about his wife, Janet, about his son, Alex, who's a handy young footballer, and daughter, Amy, who's not so bad either. About how they live in an expensive cul-de-sac of modern houses in Bramhall with a security gate at the end of the road, and how he's got a television the size of Jodrell Bank in front of which he saw two championships being won. (That's the present condition of televised football, incidentally, watching the players watching the match.) We know, too, he threw a good party the night in April 1993 when the title was first won.

'The party we had that night was the best party I've ever been involved with,' he once told me, 'partly because our families and those around us knew how important the title was to us and the sense of relief was enormous.'

He lets us know all that, he even borrows a video camera from Granada to record it all for a programme called *Captain's Log*. But anything meaty, any serious analysis of the state of Manchester United or how he really feels? No chance. Like the United Megastore, which was still charging for Andrei Kanchelskis posters three months after he deserted the club, Steve Bruce gives nothing away.

He is a man who believes in responsibility. He uses the word a lot, talking about responsibility to the fans, responsibility to his fellow players and most of all responsibility to the club. Whether it's piling in to the penalty area for a last-minute charge at goal when the team's losing, or not letting any secrets out of the bag, he remembers where his loyalties lie. He has been schooled in the new United way: keep the lid on it; don't let anyone in who's not one of us. In all areas, United's best-ever defender. Or in the upstairs downstairs cliché of football, he has been a great servant to Manchester United: the best.

And now he's gone. The 1996 season was his last in a red shirt. He has taken up Trevor Francis's invitation (not to mention David

Sullivan's soft-porn millions) to spend a twilight year or two at Birmingham City, a patient in need of a major guts transplant. You can't blame him: heart can only compensate for so much loss of speed, and his place at the centre of United's endeavours had looked increasingly less secure over his last few months. A million a year: it's not to be dismissed lightly. Besides, as Bruce himself said in his polite, reasonable and straightforward press statement to announce his departure from his adopted home, joining Birmingham and helping revive the sleeping giant was 'an opportunity I felt I had to take'.

TOP SNOG

Ryan Giggs. Life began: 4.5.91

Ulster was slipping into orange anarchy, MPs were about to plunge their noses deep into the trough and award themselves pay rises seven times the rate of inflation, Boris Yeltsin had just won the Russian election, thus sending distillers' shares up dozens of roubles on the burgeoning Moscow stock exchange. But on Sunday, 7 July 1996, *The News of the World* had no doubt about the most important story of the week. Failing to resist the punning possibilities offered by his profession, the paper's front page headline announced: 'Giggs scored four times with stripper.'

It could be gleaned, over the next three pages of intimate reminiscence about the night he took her back to his place after spotting her charms in a Mancunian club, that 19-year-old table-dancer Christina James was taken by Ryan Giggs's off-field performance. She trilled on about the way he let her take control ('I thought, me, I'm telling Ryan Giggs what to do'), cooed about his thoughtfulness ('he kept on asking if I was all right'), couldn't get over the fact they ended up in a wardrobe (his ironic response, presumably, to the Liverpool fans' old slander that he was in the closet). 'He's an absolutely brilliant kisser,' she gushed. 'He simply makes you feel so special. I hope he does get back in touch.' Keep hoping, Christina. Can't see he'll be too quick on the phone now you've shared those precious moments of privacy with seven million others.

But through all the details and frank – very frank – revelations, you couldn't help feeling *The News of the World* let us all down with their exposé of Ryan's fling. Thanks to Christina they had total, as it were, inside access and yet they failed to deliver the single piece of information we all want to know: does Ryan Giggs sleep under a Ryan Giggs duvet cover?

It is true what they say: these days top footballers get treated like royalty. Which means every indiscretion – an evening on the beer, a run of bad luck at the bookies, a night with a Manc slapper – is reported with relish by the tabloids. Indeed they don't even have to be top footballers. When Graham Roberts's marriage ran into difficulties in 1995, even though he had ceased to play for Spurs five years previously and was simply manager of non-league Yeovil Town, it was news considered worthy of a full-page investigation in *The Daily Mirror*. Like those of the royals, the private lives of our own dear football heroes have become a big commercial proposition. And in the uncompromisingly dirty war of the circulation, no proposition is bigger than Ryan Giggs. What he does sells papers: his face on the cover of a magazine has been proven to lift sales by thousands. And what he seems to do is a lot of girls. Moreover, they seem to be girls who not only find his charms irresistible, but also come over all wobbly and unnecessary at the sniff of a tabloid's cheque-book. Even the girls from his more stable relationships cannot resist the lure of publicity, telling anyone who will pay them about his skill, stamina and size.

But there is more to the reporting than simply satisfying a national thirst for prattle about the lifestyles of the rich and famous. Ryan Giggs is the boy who has everything that is reckoned to matter in the modern world: looks, youth, money. And thus there is a real longing to discover a chink in his armour. Such a discovery – that he might have feet of clay – would come as an enormous relief to the inhabitants of the sea of mediocrity swishing at his ankles. The tabloids have long since grasped this central truth about the human, or more particularly the British, psyche: for us sad inadequates with our unexceptional, unremarkable, dreary lives, to know there is a price to pay for success is news cheery enough to buy the paper for. It makes us feel a lot happier to know that Princess Diana, for all her tiaras and privileges, is so miserable she spends most of her private minutes when she's not whinnying about how she's no longer HRH with her fingers down her throat. It cheers us up no end to read about Jamie Blandford, driven to drugs by the force of all that inheritance money, poor bunny. We love it that Bestie had it all and had to drink to forget that he did. Now Giggs is the target for that search: if he's that good, we've got to find something bad to make us all feel better.

The trouble with Ryan Giggs is, however hard they try to seek out the news we want to read, the chink remains obstinately hidden. A momentary lapse of taste concerning Ms James and the occasional corner dispatched into the fifth row of the East Lower stand apart, there is apparently no flaw causing him misery and us delight. As well-balanced off the pitch as he is on it, he's polite, honest, determined, professional, decent – what my mum would call a credit to his family. And now we learn he's also a brilliant snogger. Makes you sick.

It is hard to overstate the level of Ryan Giggs's fame. It's not just all over the papers, his face is everywhere. Of the 1,500 items of merchandise available in the Manchester United Megastore, about 1,499 feature his dark, seductive features. Dozens of organisations hitch their corporate image to his star: the manufacturers of vegeburgers reckon they'll sell more if Giggsy endorses their taste-free fare, film manufacturers think we will choose their product because his face is on their advertisements. He is now so celebrated that Reebok can construct an entire television commercial, a mini epic with a budget approaching the gross national product of El Salvador, around the concept of dozens of famous people wishing that they could trade everything they have achieved for an hour in Ryan Giggs's boots. He is so big, they can risk an advert about him in which he doesn't even appear. At a time when multi-national corporations have discovered that association with football is good for them, he is the footballer they most want to be associated with. And the more his face is used in commercials, the more famous he becomes, and the more they want to be associated with him. It is a benevolent circle which has his agent chortling all the way to the cash point.

It is, however, a fame so significant it cannot but impinge on his daily round. There is not a moment in Ryan Giggs's life when he is not reminded of his celebrity: at work, rest and play. When we were filming the *United Family Tree* documentary we went to the Cliff to interview him. He didn't have long, he said, between finishing training and going off to the recording session of United's FA Cup final song – the frankly ear-threatening 'Move Move Move (The Red Tribe)' – so we set up all the lights and the camera on the vast indoor astroturf pitch there, ready for him to pop in, talk and go. One of our team waited outside the changing-room door to escort him across the car-park and to the waiting interview. It is a walk of about 100 yards and it took them nearly three-quarters of an hour. Giggs was surrounded by people seeking his autograph on magazine covers, replica shirts and the packaging of those little plastic figurines of him, to the point where he couldn't move. Everyone wanted a part of him, wanted, like Christina James, to be in close proximity to a genius. When he eventually fought his way to the indoor pitch, the workmen constructing new changing-rooms and a new gym there didn't just stop what they were doing to watch, two of them actually recorded him being interviewed on video cameras they just happened to have brought along. And then, when it had finished, one of the builders produced four cameras and asked if he could take snap-shots with all of them ('sorry, Ryan, do you mind? They're for me daughter, she's Giggsy potty, she is').

But that wasn't the end of it. The executive producer of our programme, a senior BBC staffer who has worked with many a celeb in the past without batting an eyelid, had decided that of all the interviews we had done with everyone from Bobby Charlton to Bryan Robson, this was the one she wanted to come and watch being filmed, to check on our progress. And at the end, when someone produced a polaroid camera, she asked if he minded, and had a snap taken of him and her together. It is now pinned in pride of place to the wall of her office.

What was remarkable about all this was that never once did Ryan Giggs show anything other than total patience. Like a benevolent father, he indulged us all with a preternatural calm, apparently floating above the mayhem, detached from it all, his real presence elsewhere. I thought as he left the building, signing all sorts of items proffered by the workmen, if you could bottle his demeanour you would put the Prozac corporation out of business in a week.

Ryan Giggs is comfortable with fame because, from an early age, he was so sure it would become part of his life, he prepared for it. When he was a child he used to practise his autograph. When I interviewed him for *GQ* magazine once he said that it had always been his ambition to be on its cover. And a photographer who took some of the first studio portraits of him (as Alex Ferguson once pointed out, he is a photogenic boy) said he was such a good model, it was as if he had rehearsed the role. With preparation like that, when fame arrived, he wasn't surprised or wrong-footed by it; and, now it's attached itself to him, he's rather pleased with it. One or two irritations apart.

'I used to read all the papers, every match report about me,' he told me, 'but now I don't. Once they start getting involved in your private life the best thing is to ignore them. So I don't bother.'

Honestly?

'Yeah, really. I don't read them.'

But what really pleases him about fame is that it proves he is being recognised for doing his job right. Everything flows from what he does on the pitch: get that wrong and fame will soon find another bedfellow.

Whatever else he is – model, clothes-hanger, serial skirt-chaser – Ryan Giggs is first and foremost a fantastic footballer. On 5 February 1994, against Queen's Park Rangers, he blessed all of us who were there to witness it with a goal from another planet.

It was some game, that one; an end-to-end romp of a 3–2 win, the sort of game, if you were Ryan Giggs, you'd like to take out on a date. Les Ferdinand, as he always seemed to be against United when he played for QPR, was imperious that day. He scored both of theirs, the second a shot from 25 yards executed with such minimal back lift, Peter Schmeichel hardly knew he'd hit it before it was in the back of the net. It was the type of goal that had you wishing Fergie would get his cheque-book out on the spot.

For the reds, Kanchelskis scored a cracker, and Cantona too, but the goal which stood out in a convocation of excellence was in the second half. Giggs won the ball in the centre circle and started to run, shoulders hunched, head down, ball tucked on to the toes of his left Reebok. As he ran, players seemed to fall over. He marked a dizzy, mazy, zig-zag line through the QPR defence, leaving bodies in his wash: Ray Wilkins went down, Yates and Bardsley too, and Darren Peacock, tripping over his own hair; even Mark Hughes, following his own man, fell over. It was like a cartoon from an old-style football magazine. You almost expected to see a dotted white line appearing on the pitch to mark the course of the run. And the final player to fall over was the keeper, who dived and missed the concluding shot, as it tucked itself cosily into the net's corner.

But Giggs didn't realise at the time what he was doing. 'I just put my head down and went for it,' he told me when I asked him about it once. 'I honestly thought I had a free run at goal. It was only when I watched it on *Match of the Day* that night that I saw what I'd done. I thought: where'd he come from?'

It was a goal Alex Ferguson enjoyed just a bit, as well. 'Ryan's powers of control at speed are due to his incredible balance,' Fergie explained at the time. 'He can wrong-foot anybody just by a movement and when you think a tackler is going to get a foot to the ball, he seems to float or ride or roll over the challenge. The defender always seems to go down, while the lad stays on his feet.'

There was something else about that goal: it was old-fashioned. Not just in the cut of Giggs's Stanley Matthews memorial baggy black away shorts, but in the execution of it. It was brave and reckless and not something players have dared risk for 25 years in a game of increasing pressure. It was like something Jimmy Greaves might have done. Or Bestie.

The comparison has been in the air ever since Ryan Giggs emerged. But the similarities on the pitch are compelling. You can see it in the Bestian slope of the shoulders, the way he addresses the ball, the way he drifts across the turf without apparent effort. But, unlike George, Giggs will never let it slip; there's going to be no pissing it up against the wall there. Rarely has there been a more single-minded approach to a God-given talent as Ryan Giggs's: from the start he knew he was good, and he would do anything he could to improve on and exploit that talent to maximise his potential. Even turning up to training. 'I enjoy training,' he told me. 'I feel frustrated if I come away from a session and haven't learned something.'

Alex Ferguson loves that about him. 'He has such a wonderful attitude, such a desire to realise the greatness that is within him,' he once said. 'And it's up to us at the club to assist his development. He is a thinker about the game and a listener, no question about that. Ryan has a shit-disposal unit in his head and much of what he hears goes into that. But if something is useful or valid, he'll store it away for the future.'

That ability to learn, and the appetite to better himself which has sometimes led to his female conquests to complain to the press that he is more interested in a night in studying videos of the great strikers than he is going out to a paparazzi-patrolled restaurant, has been evident from the start: if you want fame you work at it. Giggs's history has been well-chronicled; nonetheless it tells important truths. The fact his dad – Danny Wilson, the brilliant rugby league player – was a bad boy of Bestian proportions who eventually deserted his young family, has imbued Giggs with a sense of real responsibility. Not just towards his mother, whom he plainly adores, whose maiden name he took and for whom he chose to play for Wales. But also to his craft and his club. When Alex Ferguson called at his door with Joe Brown, United's youth development officer, and signed him up as a schoolboy from under Manchester City's nose (the pleasure doesn't dilute with the retelling of that anecdote), the boss knew. He knew that, though the boy was only 14 years old, he had the attitude to make it.

'You just knew from the moment he walked on the pitch this was a player,' said Ferguson, who is second to none in his ability to spot talent. 'The way he moved, it was like a gazelle, lovely to watch.'

And if they loved him at United, the feelings were reciprocated. 'I'd stood on the Stretford End as a kid,' he said. 'They were me heroes, Sparky, Robbo. And to be like, you know, queuing up for food in the canteen with Robbo, I was really nervous and excited.'

He was reckoned ready from an early age and was propelled on a speedy conveyor belt to fame. No hanging around, he tore through the junior teams a bit like he did through QPR's defence that time. 'I think the first senior player I spoke to was Viv Anderson,' he remembered. 'I was put in a five-a-side at training with some of the first-team squad and I went past him about four or five times. The next time I went past him, he kicked me. So the first thing any senior player said to me was probably "sorry, son" as he picked me up from the ground.'

Next thing you know, Viv Anderson's on his way out to Sheffield Wednesday and Giggs was in the first team. He came on as substitute in a 2–0 away defeat at Everton on 26 March 1991 and made his debut against Manchester City at Old Trafford on 4 May 1991. The team that day was as follows: Walsh, Irwin, Blackmore, Bruce, Phelan, Pallister, Robson, Webb, McClair, Hughes, Giggs

(Donaghy); the crowd was 45,286; the score 1–0 and the scorer Giggs.

'I didn't really score it,' he told me. 'It was a goalmouth scramble. It hit me, then hit someone else, then hit Colin Hendry and went in. It was an own goal, but the defender didn't want to take responsibility. It was my debut so the boss told the press I'd got it. I was 17, I wasn't going to argue.'

He played 40 games in the 1992 league campaign and that was a learning experience if ever there was one. That year he may have been the youngest player ever to win the PFA Young Player award, and he may have popped a Rumbelows Cup winner's medal into the cabinet in the room his mum keeps as a sort of ever-expanding Ryan Giggs museum at the cottage in Worsley where he grew up. But so what. What he learnt most from that season is that he was part of the team that lost the title. When he left the ground the day it ended at Anfield, a couple of Liverpool fans asked him for his autograph, and then when he obliged – he'd put in the homework for that moment, after all – the pair of Scouse wits tore it up and threw the paper in his face, shouting 'loser'. What hurt a competitor like him about that was that they were right.

'It was awful, losing it at Liverpool,' he said. 'I hated it, but it didn't really strike me how much it meant to other people until I went away on holiday and everywhere I went I met people saying: "Are we ever going to do it?" And you could see how much it meant to them.'

He put it in that memory bank of his: getting that close and blowing it hurts. He wouldn't let it happen again.

In the first few months of the double-winning season of 1993–94 Giggs was supreme, a counter-attacking missile, fired off by Cantona, a colleague, he said, who seemed to be able to judge exactly how fast a full-back could run when he threaded through a ball. Scoring became so commonplace (he hit 17 in the season) he developed a celebration which involved walking away from the goal uninterested, face set in an impassive neutral, finger wagging as if he was ticking off a fractious infant. A radio commentator observed on one occasion when he had just moped off after scoring a blistering goal, that his lack of joy showed he had fallen out of love with the game. Which shows that too much Freudian analysis is not helpful when dealing with footballers. Giggs was just being a lad.

'Celebrations have got well out of hand,' he said at the time. 'The best celebrations are the simple ones, cool ones. Cole, Shearer, Ian Wright – you've got to have respect for Ian Wright. I'm trying to do a celebration which isn't.'

His favourite piece of non-celebration that year was in the away game at Leeds United which followed Mark Hughes's semi-final against Oldham. It was a vital game for United's title effort; Elland Road was an indomitable place to visit, but United needed a win: to secure points, to steady their own nerves and to set Blackburn's jangling. It was in doubt until five minutes from the end, Kanchelskis's opener just hadn't looked enough as Leeds attacked and attacked, as Bruce, Pallister, Irwin and Schmeichel battled and scrambled. But then Giggs, out on the touchline, beat Gary Kelly, the Irish full-back who had got the better of him during the fixture at Old Trafford, for the first time that night. He spun inside to play a one-two with Hughes, who was still flying after his semi-final volley. When Giggs scored from the perfect return pass, he stood absolutely still, face expressionless, as if rooted to the penalty spot. Then he was buried under a human tower-block of celebration – Roy Keane, as always, forming the top floor.

'He liked that one,' Paul Ince said at the time. 'At Old Trafford people were saying Kelly had him in his pocket and I think he felt as like he had a point to prove. When he scored that goal he thought, yeah, up yours, so he done the Chris Eubank bit.'

'I loved it,' Giggs, the true red, said. 'I always seem to do well at Elland Road, which is pretty pleasing really because they hate us so much. You go to take a corner and there's 10,000 skinheads in their end screaming murder at you. It's nice to do well.'

Medals were not the only thing Giggs picked up in that triumphant year, however. In its latter stages, for the first time in his career, he got injured. He had a tonsil problem that winter which sapped his energy and led to a Manc rumour that he had contracted ME – Giggsy flu. It may have been that which slowed him fractionally, and meant he got caught and started to collect niggles: hamstrings, tendon problems, a knee knock. I interviewed him once around that time, and what I couldn't get over were his feet. He was sitting in his mum's house, and had kicked off his trainers as we talked. Off the field he rarely wears socks and his feet were there on full display. He has incredible, finger-length toes which he curls round as he speaks. Each one carried evidence of that season: blackened and chipped nails, unnatural bends and callouses, a vociferous scar across one heel. They looked instruments in need of a long period of recovery. In the euphoric rush at the end of that season, not many noticed that his form was sliding. If they did, they just thought like me: he's young, he's exhausted, he should spend a month with his feet in a bucket of cold water.

Until he started the 1994–95 defence of the double, that is. After scoring twice against Gothenburg in an early Champions League game, his form didn't just dip, it packed its bags and ran off with someone else, a case of desertion that warranted an investigation by the CSA. He couldn't cross, he couldn't run, he couldn't beat a full-back. And he certainly couldn't score: clean through time and again he would fire it straight at the goalkeeper. He only managed four all year. In the stands, the fans began to moan. Ferguson may be a loyal man, but this was loyalty too far, they moaned, the lad was becoming a liability. They'd rather see Sharpe on the United left than Giggs: that's how bad it was.

His nadir came in the Barcelona game. I talked to him at the airport when the party arrived in the city and he was hanging around waiting for the luggage to be unloaded. He was as friendly as ever, with a firm handshake and that big smile that completely transforms his otherwise solemn features. He looked relaxed, said he felt good, said he was looking forward to it. The press party seemed to share his optimism. Patrick Barclay, *The Sunday Telegraph*'s doyen, conducted a sweep on the plane to see what we thought the score would be. Of 22 of us he polled, only two predicted a Barcelona victory. Me, I thought it would be 2–1 to United, with Giggs getting the winner to show the world, on this world stage, who was tops.

But at training in the Nou Camp the night before the match, when Mick Hucknall joined in and scored past Gary Walsh (it was an omen Ferguson didn't heed) we should have realised. Giggsy looked hopeless. He couldn't trap the ball, every pass he received seemed to bounce off his shins, every pass he gave was a couple of feet short of accuracy. The word you kept hearing him say that night in training was 'sorry'. If anything, in the game itself on the night of 2 November 1994, in front of 114,432 people, he was worse. He looked lost. Nothing he tried came off and by the end of the game he had nothing left to try.

In the post-match analysis Giggs's performance offered endless opportunity for the English fan's favourite pastime: self-flagellation. We thought he was the real thing, but we were deluding ourselves. Barcelona had the real thing – Stoichkov and Romario – and they came from a different place, destroying United with a performance which will rate, for those who witnessed it, as the greatest they have ever seen by a club side. Everything they touched went right. Everything our boy touched went wrong. In comparison he looked a football half-wit.

Giggs's case was not helped at that time by the fact the Giggs industry was moving into full swing. After a couple of years in which Alex Ferguson had built a wall around him, not even letting him speak to poor old Motty after *Match of the Day*, he had been let loose. The silence had done his image no harm. It made him not just a pretty face, but a mysterious one. A dozen magazine interviews were sold on the back of that, 'The Boy Wonder Speaks Out at Last' was a typical headline. And United themselves, or their merchandise wing at least, knew the strength of this brand they had on their hands. He was pushed with a relentless determinism, the radiator mascot on the United juggernaut. Reebok, too, his major sponsors, were getting their money's worth: he turned up for a public appearance in a sports shop in Swansea and 10,000 people came along for a glimpse. It didn't matter that Alex Ferguson was still keeping tabs, restricting his engagements, telling him which interviews he could undertake and which he couldn't, the sheer scale of his presence suggested he had lost sight of the football in pursuit of the fame. Even his mum, he told me, got fed up of the sight of him peering down from every hoarding and every magazine rack every time she went out shopping.

The press loved it. It wasn't just the tabloids who tried to lever a crowbar into the apparent chink in the golden boy's defence. *The Independent* ran an article wondering if he'd blown it and suggested the way his hair kept getting in his eyes was symbolic. *The Guardian* compared him with Steve McManaman and found him wanting: Giggs was nothing but a flash, an overmarketed, overhyped empty vessel, the paper reckoned. Macca, on the other hand, was a determinist who was going to let no frip or fop get in his way (this was, remember, before McManaman turned up at the 1996 Cup final in an oufit apparently tailored for a Brixton pimp).

In the stands, the fans turned noisy, quick to apportion blame. His then girlfriend, Dani Behr, gave up watching him because of the abuse she took every time she went along to Old Trafford: 'He's knackered himself shagging you,' some gent once informed her. Even the passionate and partisan United fanzine writer Richard Kurt lost his belief. He included in his predictions for the 1995–96 season penned in the last *Red Issue* of 1994–95 the following prophecy: 'Ryan Giggs retires from football to take over from Robbie in Take That.'

Which summed it up nicely.

We were all wrong. That season he hadn't been undermined by his spending too much time exploiting his image. After all it only takes an afternoon to sit for enough photos to overtake the Princess of Wales in the magazine-cover handicap chase. And it may come as a surprise, but he didn't spend his every waking minute sweating over a word-processor writing *Ryan Giggs: My Story* (which gave him a record, incidentally, as the youngest sportsman ever to publish an autobiography). That was constructed by some sad hack in need of a couple of grand to pay a tax bill. No, it was the injuries that did for his form. What we all underestimated was how bad those injuries had been, how debilitating the knocks evident by a quick glance at his feet had proven. In the trench warfare of modern football, you don't give your enemies psychological advantage by revealing how messed-up your major weapons are. With Cantona in self-imposed exile, United couldn't afford to lose Giggs as well, so he was patched up and thrown into the fray time and again when what he needed was a lengthy break and space to rehabilitate. 'I couldn't go two games without picking up another knock,' he said of that time. 'It was horrible, really.'

But it wasn't just the injuries that had been underestimated. Few had appreciated the strength of Giggs's character, either, too busy writing him off as a fly-by-night to see the steely edge beneath the swirling locks. What he was doing all year was not wasting time, but working. Working on his game, working on his fitness, working to see if improving his technique might give him the confidence to run at a full-back again. He watched Eric Cantona in training and thought if someone like him has to work at it, none of us is good enough to rest on our laurels. You could see his effort in the 1995 Cup final. United had finally accepted the inevitable, and he had been out for nearly a month with yet another injury. That day he was restricted to sitting on the bench. But when he came on, he tore at Everton, trying, trying, trying. In the end it wasn't enough, and Everton won the attrition. But no one at that game could suggest that Ryan Giggs let them down.

And so in 1995–96, after time to sort himself out, to rest, to let the United physio get at him, Giggs was ready, prepared as ever. He'd overcome his injuries and was happy to go out and establish himself once again. He did more than that: he proved to be better than we had previously thought possible. He had a great season, a dream team of a year: not just a mercurial presence on the wing, but a player ready to take control of a game, to dominate it. Perversely, the departures of Andrei Kanchelskis and his mate and minder Paul Ince plus the elevation of Paul Scholes, Nicky Butt, David Beckham and the Neville boys may have helped him. Not one to side-step responsibility, he realised that at 22 he was now a veteran in the side, and had to be in charge. He moved inside a fraction to midfield and his passing and his crossing, those things he had worked on in his lean time, began to show the effort.

All that, plus, from October, the fact Eric Cantona returned. With his hero back, spurred on by Cantona's touch and go, Giggs scored 11 goals in the year. And when he did score, gone was the nonchalant wag of the finger; he celebrated them like he thought he'd never score again. In the derby at Maine Road, after a 30-yarder had hit the stanchion in the back of the net with such force it had bounced out almost immediately, thus confusing the United fans into silence, he ran half-way back to Old Trafford in delight before spread-eagling himself in satisfaction under the excited bodies of his team-mates, his face alight in a schoolboy beam of happiness.

Typically, if, at the end of his best-ever season in a United shirt, Ryan Giggs was tempted to cock two fingers at his detractors, he wasn't showing it. When I caught up with him and we spoke on the vast, plastic expanse of the Cliff's indoor pitch (he was wearing at the time a blister-inducing combination of new black Oxford shoes and no socks) he remembered the first thing about media presentation he had been told during the lessons the club had given him in the years Alex Ferguson shielded him from public inquiry: be friendly, be polite, be bland. But whatever the professional demeanour, he couldn't disguise the icy glint which runs through his veins. When I asked him if it got a little boring, winning all the time, if reaching 22 years of age with three league championships and two FA Cup wins already to his name meant he'd fulfilled all his ambitions, he looked at me as if I really had lost the plot.

'I love winning,' he said. 'When you're winning, you just can't see yourself losing, only winning. When you get a little taste of success you just want more and more. You just get more confident and then you get better and then you win more.'

And then he smiled. At which you realised that Christina James and the tabloid press really have no chance. Ryan Giggs has only got room for one mistress in his life, and nothing – not fame, not girls, not appearing on *Top of the Pops* looking embarrassed miming to a crap dance record – is going to distract him from pursuit of the most intense pleasure of all. Victory.

YOU KNOW WHAT THEY SAY
ABOUT BIG HANDS

Peter Schmeichel. Life began: 17.8.91

On the evening of Monday, 4 March 1996, it seemed like the whole of Newcastle was going to the game. Newcastle against Manchester United, reckoned the championship-decider, had been whipped up by a football-ravenous media to the point where it left a heavy knot of expectation in the stomach. Everywhere you looked, people were flooding through the town, heading towards St James's Park, which sits on top of a hill just north of the city centre, its grey concrete sides steepling up from the surrounding streets, a cathedral calling the citizenry to worship. Even if they didn't have tickets, the locals were on their way to the pubs on the stadium's apron, to watch it on the telly, anxious just to be close.

It was a freezing night, a wind biting in direct from the Urals, but no one wore a coat. It was as if to do so was to compromise your commitment to the cause. Everyone was dressed for their part in the proceedings in replica Toon shirts. Queues stretched from every pub doorway, beyond which you could see a bouncing, throbbing heave of black and white striped nylon, a sight to make Adidas executives' hearts sing.

In one bar, just opposite the ground, confidence was rising as pints were sunk, suffocating any hint of doubt. Men in black and white stripes sang the praises of Ginola, Ferdinand and, to the signature tune of the old Rupert the Bear cartoon, 'Philippe, Philippe Albert; everyone knows his name'. To express anything other than certainty in a Toon victory here, now, was to let the lads down. A couple of fans I talked to were definite that Asprilla, the Colombian bought

145

recently for £6 million to add the final championship-winning gloss, would score and they could witness at first hand his cartwheel goal celebration. It was just, they reckoned, a matter of what minute of the game he would strike.

'First or last would do me,' one of them said.

'Youse Man U?' the other asked.

I said I was.

'Well, youse might as well go home now.'

Newcastle had won every game at home all season, they added. Well, except for the recent FA Cup tie against Chelsea, but the cup didn't matter; this was the league. And the league, they reckoned, had Wor Kev's name on it. 'Mind you,' said one of them, as he slid the last of his pint down his throat and headed off to the stadium. 'Youse lot are a canny team.'

Inside the ground, black and white stripes filled every cranny. Except for one wedge in the corner, where 3,000 United fans, sensibly wrapped in Paul and Shark yachting jackets against the chill, broke the uniformity. But the Geordies were up for this one, no question. The noise that broke as the two teams strode on to the pitch was the loudest I'd ever heard at a league game. Andy Cole – back in Newcastle for the first time since his transfer and generously greeted by the home fans when he trotted out for the warm-up – theatrically put his fingers in his ears against the row. And yet it got louder as Newcastle poured at United from the kick-off, a blitz breaking about red heads. After five minutes, as Ginola, Asprilla and Ferdinand tore forward, playing with a passion and power apparently sucked direct from the stands, you knew how General Custer must have felt, knowing the end was close at hand, that nothing you could do was going to stop this.

Eighty-five minutes later, at the final whistle, St James's Park was silent. Except, that is, for a dancing, chanting, swirling, multi-coloured corner. Eric Cantona had volleyed the only goal of the game in the 51st minute, slipping into the space vacated by a Newcastle full-back who had been dragged forward by the noise, meeting Phil Neville's masterful cross-field pass and sending United's fans into a celebratory stew. Like the Geordies, the reds knew what it meant, how important this game was. It was the defeat which planted a debilitating parasite of doubt in Newcastle's title hopes.

They had been at one stage 12 points clear at the top of the league, at which planning had started for the celebration party, the biggest in Newcastle history. A man had spent £2,000 commissioning a giant flag to hang off one of the several bridges across the Tyne proclaiming 'Newcastle, Champions 1996'. But United, steady, undemonstrative, calm-headed, had tacked them back. Now they had come to Newcastle's fortress home and absorbed all the blood and thunder Kevin Keegan's team could throw at them. When you play as well as Newcastle had and lose, you start to worry if it's not all over. And though Cantona had got the goal, there was one man chiefly responsible for the tears which began to prick Geordie eyes: Peter Schmeichel, the goalkeeper who snatched a championship.

Tommy Docherty maintains that United would have won the title in 1976 under his stewardship if the then famously parsimonious board had met the player's wage demands and allowed him to sign Peter Shilton from Leicester. If that sounds like post-rationalisation taken to new levels of whining, it is worth remembering that when Shilton joined Nottingham Forest a year later, they won the championship and thence the European Cup twice. Goalkeepers win you things, as Kevin Keegan now knows. In his overexcited moments of self-justification towards the end of the 1996 season, Keegan said that he would never renounce his attacking principles, he'd rather walk out of the job than win the title defensively. Admirable sentiments, except that no matter how persuasive your attack, you will never win the league when your full-backs are overcome by wanderlust or when your goalkeeper flaps at a soft shot like an injured bird and lets in a goal in the last minute of a game against Blackburn which you have to win at all costs.

David Seaman proved it in Euro 96: when you have a presence between the posts, the psychological advantage is yours. Schmeichel as good as won United the title that night in Newcastle. In the first five minutes, once from Asprilla and twice from Ferdinand, he produced three saves which tore the heart from their endeavour. You could see it on Ferdinand's face; he couldn't believe it. Put through on his own, he struck his shots cleanly, crisply, hard for the corner. But Schmeichel, leaping towards him at speed, limbs everywhere, reducing the huge acreage of the open goal down to nothing, got something to it – hand, wrist, forearm, it was so quick you couldn't really tell – and the chance was gone. Ferdinand stopped for a moment, on his knees, and stared, and you could see him thinking: we'll never beat these.

That's Schmeichel's trademark: a save he has developed he calls the star jump. He flings himself at the shooting player, arms and legs akimbo, spreading himself into a huge security blanket for the United goal. It doesn't matter which bit of the body the ball hits – against Manchester City he once saved a screamer with his cheekbone – the point is just to get something in the way. It's not pretty, and when it doesn't work he is left looking foolish, sitting on the ground, legs at 90 degrees underneath him like a big rag doll on the nursery floor. But it has proven far more effective than a handsome dive. It is as significant an advance in the goalkeeper's art as it was for high jumpers the day Dick Fosbury ran up to the pole backwards.

Unlike Keegan, Alex Ferguson never underestimated the importance of goalkeepers. When he came down from Aberdeen, he found Gary Bailey on the point of retirement and Chris Turner spending most of his games retrieving balls from the back of the net which had been chipped over his head. Fergie thought it best, then, to bring Jim Leighton with him. Bandy-legged and with the face of an extra from *Night of the Living Dead,* Leighton was alleged to be the Scottish goalkeeper who gave the lie to all those jokes about Scottish goalkeepers. The 1990 FA Cup final suggested otherwise. In a dire display, Leighton wafted at the ball with as much style and effect as those bird men who jump off Bognor pier every year. Crystal Palace popped three past him, the third Ian Wright almost missed, so astonished was he to be parcelled such a gift on the far post. Before the replay, Alex Ferguson did what the burgeoning Old Trafford fanzine movement had been suggesting for two years he should do and dropped Leighton. The two men were friends; they'd been through much together; it was a horrible thing to do, Ferguson reckoned, the hardest personal decision he has faced in management. But in his frame of reference nothing can come in the way of the collective enterprise, certainly not sentiment. For a while it destroyed Leighton's career; it took him two years and a return to Scotland to rebuild his confidence sufficiently to put him in his country's squad for Euro 96.

Not that we on the terraces cared much, particularly after Les Sealey, on loan from Luton, saved a free kick in the first five minutes of the replay, the kind of shot which Leighton, recently behaving like a traffic cop on point duty, would have waved into the back of the goal. We loved Sealey for that and then for the dignity he showed in offering Leighton his medal afterwards, and for turning down a nice pay-day from a tabloid seeking his story. We loved him, too, when he stayed on for another year, for the fury he showed when Jimmy McGregor suggested he came off after a collision in the 1991 Rumbelows Cup final. 'I'm not coming off,' you could see him yelling, this despite the fact there was a stud cut so deep on the knee his bone was exposed. We loved him even more for his bravery in the Cup Winners' Cup final six weeks later, when he was waiting to undertake the random drug test after the game and Julio Salinas, Barcelona's chosen player, took one look at the ghastly scar on his knee and, never mind urine, almost provided a vomit sample.

But we weren't wholly surprised when Alex Ferguson moved in the summer of 1991 for the Danish international keeper Peter Schmeichel. However much you loved him, you couldn't help feeling Sealey was a couple of branches short of the top of the tree.

Short is not a word you would associate with Peter Schmeichel. At £500,000 from the Danish club Bronby, Schmeichel must be, £ for lb, the best buy United have ever made, not least because at 6ft 4ins and 14 stone they got an awful lot of pounds for their money. The son of a Polish professional pianist and a Danish musician, Schmeichel brought with him a pair of hands that looked anything but the dainty, delicate digits of an instrumentalist. They were huge, like he was permanently wearing those foam pointy finger things the crowd wave at the recording of *Gladiators*. The day he made his debut on 17 August 1991, at home to Notts County, his hands alone seemed to fill the goal. The team then was: Schmeichel, Irwin, Blackmore, Bruce, Ferguson (Giggs), Parker, Robson, Ince (Pallister), McClair, Hughes, Kanchelskis; the score was 2–0; the scorers Hughes ('Youzeh') and Robson; the crowd 45,286. And it was immediately clear this white-haired giant of a keeper, greeted with a reworking of Monty Python's Viking drinking song from the stands as he kept a clean sheet in his first four games, was the business.

There is a magnificent picture of Schmeichel, taken some time in 1993 and turned into a jigsaw by the Manchester United merchandising department about three days later, which shows him at his most majestic. He is hanging, horizontal, in the air, spread across his goal, a vast hand wrapped round the ball which is clearly, whoever struck it believes, heading for the top right-hand corner. Remarkably for such a bizarre and unnatural pose, the keeper's eyes are open, a model of concentration, looking straight and true at the ball. And so too is his mouth. Wide open. What you realise after a couple of seconds looking at this picture is that when it was taken, Peter Schmeichel was flying through the air, shouting.

From the moment he stationed himself comfortably and confidently between United's posts, kicking the base of each one superstitiously before every game, the noise this son of a Polish soloist made was hardly of a classical note. He quickly assimilated into his Danish vocabulary a range of ripe examples of English vernacular which he unleashed at everyone who came within earshot. And many who didn't.

Schmeichel swears at a phenomenal rate on a football pitch; his output would bring a blush to Roy 'Chubby' Brown. When he found himself behind Steve Bruce, who similarly favours full and frank debate, the two were at each other's throats all game, every game. Never mind that Bruce had been so hospitable to Schmeichel when he first arrived at Old Trafford that the two of them ended up living next door to each other, they yelled and bawled and screamed, holding each other responsible for every defensive mishap. It became a feature of United's play; once I was standing behind the goal when Gary Walsh was understudying Schmeichel and I thought the whole game looked slower, United less committed, less interested. Then I realised, with the polite young Walsh in position, that it was because no one was yelling at one another.

Schmeichel claims he bawls to keep the adrenalin fired in the periods of langour between saves. 'It's my way of feeding my energy into my concentration,' he told Ian Stafford in *The Independent* the week of the 1996 Cup final. 'Although, believe me, Bruce and Pallister are no angels either. Don't forget you only ever get to see me shouting at them because, when they do it to me, their backs are turned. Being a goalkeeper means you have to concentrate all the time, but I don't go round in everyday life abusing people. It is like I am two different people.' Which is just as well. Imagine him out and about on the streets, in a sort of permanent goal rage.

When there's no one about to shout at, Schmeichel does other things to keep himself occupied, like conducting the singing in the crowd or like winding up those sitting in the Kop at Liverpool (not such a smart idea, that one in the 1996 meeting, as a few minutes after doing it he was picking the ball out of the net twice). Or like charging at the fan who invaded the pitch during the European Cup game at Old Trafford against Galatasaray in 1993, and bundling him so ferociously off the field the guy ended up in the fourth row of the North stand.

'He was a Turk, came on with a burning United flag,' Schmeichel explained at the press conference after that game. 'You never know what he was intending, he came from behind us all and I saw him first. It was frustration really that made me do it. We were losing and you don't know if the referee is going to add time for this sort of thing, so I wanted him off the pitch quickly. That's all.'

A Turkish journalist in the throng challenged this version of events. 'He was not a Turkish fan,' he said. 'He was a Kurd, burning a Turkish flag. This was political.' Schmeichel didn't accept this. 'It was a red, white and black United flag he was burning.'

'No,' said the man. 'It was a Turkish flag. He was a Kurd.'

'Well then,' said Schmeichel in his strange mix of South Manchester and South Copenhagen. 'They'll love me in Istanbul, won't they, beating up a Kurd.'

If Schmeichel appears loud on the pitch, to see him training is to see a manifestation of the maxim that to be a goalkeeper you must be unhinged. There is a sequence United, like many teams, undertake in training which involves the full-backs and midfielders crossing and the rest of the team shooting at the goal. No lengthy periods of lay-off for him, then, the goalkeeper is at the centre of things, forced into saves every second. Yet Schmeichel yells and bawls as mightily as ever. He hoots sarcastically at Denis Irwin for posting a cross straight into his hands, sneers at David Beckham for putting a shot straight into his midriff, and when he misses an Eric Cantona pile-driver, he screams at himself. The more the other players turn on him, treating him as the butt of the session, and the more Roy Keane tries to kick the ball as hard as possible directly at him, to inflict pain, the more excitable and energised he gets. Peter Schmeichel just loves to be the centre of attention.

As a keeper, though, Schmeichel gave United more than just a sensational shot-stopper and a busybody Mr Angry at the back. His arm and his quickness of thought combined to add a searing counter-attacking thrust to the side. Once he picked up the ball, he would dash to the edge of the area and bowl it with a quarter-back's precision to players lurking on the half-way line. One goal he conjured against QPR at Loftus Road took – I timed it off the telly – precisely nine seconds from the moment he chucked it towards Kanchelskis's feet till the moment the Ukranian had deposited it in the Rangers net. Nine seconds to get from one end of the pitch to the other, nine seconds to travel 100 yards: route one at its most devastating. Sometimes he will make his run to the area's edge, ball in hand, elbow triggered ready to fire, and find no one in the position he wants them to be. And then do they get an earful. 'Peter Schmeichel?' smiled Giggs when I asked him about the ear-melt he experiences every other game. 'No comment.'

When things are going really badly for United, Schmeichel is not content merely to fling the ball in the direction of the opponent's goal, however. He will fling himself. When the team are trailing with a few minutes to go, he bundles up into the opposition area when a corner or free kick is awarded. I have seen him go walkabout three times for the reds, with varying degrees of success. Against Everton in the 1995 FA Cup final he went up there, but on a day like that, when nothing went right, the corner was nodded easily away by the defence and he found himself in a desperate sprint challenge back to his own goal like the one he lost against the Croats when playing for Denmark in Euro 96.

Against Wimbledon in the league in 1994, with the reds trailing 1–0 and three minutes remaining, he was luckier, and got his big blond head to a corner. Unfortunately, Steve Bruce was lining up a perfectly angled approach to the same ball, and when he found it had been snatched from his forehead by his own goalkeeper, the row, as the two of them galloped back home, registered on the Richter Scale.

Against Rotor Volograd in the UEFA Cup in September 1995, though, Schmeichel's intervention was significantly more important. Never in 38 years of competition had United lost at home in Europe: Milan, Barcelona, Real Madrid, Red Star Belgrade, Juventus, Ajax, none of them had got a win at Old Trafford. And there the reds were, with three minutes left of the second leg remaining, trailing 2–1 to a team no one had heard of before the draw was made. When a corner was won, up lumbered the keeper. The ball arced towards the penalty spot, and there he was, luminous lime shirt standing out head and shoulders above the saner tones around him. It wasn't that he leapt like a salmon to be in that position; you might, were you lucky, have been able to slip a sheet of newspaper between his heels and the turf on that occasion. It was just he was naturally head and shoulders above the rest. The ball found the vast expanse of his forehead, and bounced straight into the goal.

This made him the first ever United goalkeeper to score from open play (Alex Stepney got his two in the 1973–74 season from penalties). And how did Peter Schmeichel celebrate his moment of history? He ran back to his position, yelling at his colleagues that it wasn't his job to score the bloody goals, it was theirs.

The 1995–96 season was Schmeichel's best, though, not just because of that goal. Time and again, match after match, he got himself in the way of certainties. Every time he did, he fed opponents' doubts. And the odd catastrophic error he was prone to earlier in his United career – not punching away cleanly, letting the ball slip out of his hands – became less and less frequent to the point of non-existence.

Intriguingly he believes his form was due to United being less dominant in games than they had been in the previous couple of seasons. By necessity he was more involved, and the more involved he was, the less recourse he needed to artificial ways to keep his concentration up. As a goalkeeper, nothing, he reckons, helps you make saves like making a lot of saves.

'Other seasons I've gone 20 minutes without a save,' he told Ian Stafford. 'And that, believe it or not, makes it a lot harder for you to concentrate. This time, though, I've been a lot more active. It took a little time for the youngsters to settle down and there were times when more experienced players in the team had to play out of their skins to pull us through.' He was right. When Kevin Pilkington deputised for him midway through the season, the young reserve let in ten goals in four and a half games.

All Schmeichel's importance to the team was there, on show, in that game in Newcastle. Only once before had I seen United subjected to assault like they were for the first half-hour that night, and that was when they played Barcelona at the Nou Camp in November 1994. But there was one difference between the two occasions. In Spain, Alex Ferguson, dropping one of the biggest howlers of his United career, had decided that his goalkeeper was not to be one of his three permitted foreigners. Poor Gary Walsh, stepping into the huge hole in the United goal vacated by Schmeichel, might have developed sciatica so often did he stoop to pick the ball out of the net. In Newcastle, Schmeichel was there. Time and again. Attack after attack.

After the game, my Geordie mate Nick took me and Andy Mitten, editor of *United We Stand*, out on the town. It was a Monday night, but the place was heaving. Everyone had been anticipating a championship party; instead it was a championship wake. In the clubs along the Bigg Market, where the barmaids wear beach gear and the pints cost less than a quid, the lads stood in their black and white shirts, staring into their beer, shaking their heads in disbelief. 'If we had Schmeichel,' said Nick, voicing the consensus, 'we'd have had it won by now.'

Later on, about two in the morning, we were walking down the High Street, when we saw two Toon fans in wheelchairs striped in black and white, wheeling themselves down the middle of the road. As they made their way towards a gap in the crash barriers which would allow them back on to the pavement, a car came up rapidly behind them, its driver braked more dramatically than was strictly necessary and started parping his horn intemperately at them. One of the wheelchair-bound turned round and flicked the driver a V-sign, at which point the car passenger wound down his window, leant out and shouted: 'Just cos youse in a wheelchair doesn't mean I'm not gonna give youse a good slapping.'

In response, the man in the wheelchair, showing a sprinter's turn of pace, spun up to the car and punched him through the open window. The passenger retaliated, and the two of them started trading slugs, through the window, both of them from the seated position. Within seconds the driver, the other bloke in a wheelchair, several passers-by and another bloke in a chair who had appeared from nowhere, were engaged in a frenzy of push, shove and haymaker. And I thought, as I watched a flailing, fuming man in a wheelchair, that though football may be important to them, it was good to see the Geordies putting into perspective losing the league title and getting on with their normal, everyday lives so quickly.

THE LEADER OF OUR
FOOTBALL TEAM

Eric Cantona. Life began: 12.12.92

Those of us who were there at the most significant moment in Eric Cantona's career just couldn't believe what we saw. It was a grey January evening, a league match in one of the less salubrious, less hospitable quarters of Greater London. Our hero, King Eric, the crowned head of state at Old Trafford, had been kicked in the first minute of the match, kicked in the 12th, splattered on to the turf in the 28th. This is what happens when you are Eric Cantona. The instruction is delivered to defenders in opposing teams: hit him early, rattle him, get him off. And, early in the second half, it all seemed to be going to their plan. A kick, a snarl, a hack of retaliation, a scrum of players and the referee making his way towards the protagonists, pulling the red card ostentatiously from his breast pocket. Then the pleading look, the shrug and the lonely walk, alone, towards a premature appointment with the bath water.

And then, just when you thought the whole dismal, depressing, dreary episode had run its course, something extraordinary happened. As if from nowhere Eric Cantona decided to ensure his own version of justice was upheld. He launched himself into the fray . . . and stood between Julian Dicks and Andy Cole who had a fist in each other's throats and were fuming about Nicky Butt's sending-off for retaliation in the 70th minute of the match between West Ham and Manchester United. Cantona was in there, all conciliatory and dignified, like Harry Enfield's Scouser, telling them to calm down, eh, grow up, lads, it was, after all, only a game. And in the stands, you thought: blimey, Eric the Peacemaker. That's a turn-up.

Well, wasn't that the most significant? Or are you thinking of Selhurst Park, 25 January 1995, when, sent off for the fifth time in United's myriad colours, he took a diversion to the changing-room across the chest of a South London bigot? Or the afternoon of 23 March 1995 when, in Croydon Magistrates Court, Mrs Jean Pearch gave him a sentence of two weeks imprisonment for that assault and told the prison warders to take him to the cells 'forthwith'? Or there was the morning a week later in the crown court when, after his appeal against sentence was successful and Cantona was asked by those attending a press conference whether he had any statement to make, he replied: 'When the seagulls follow the trawler it is because they think sardines will be thrown into the sea.' Or do you mean Wembley, May 11 1996, when he scored the winner in the FA Cup final and became the first foreign captain ever to lift the trophy? Not to mention the night of 9 May 1996, at the Grosvenor House Hotel in London, when he picked up his award as Footballer of the Year, told the assembled soccer scribes that he likes to flush criticism round the U-bend and the representatives of *The Sun*, in a classic piece of Freudian misunderstanding, thought he was calling them toilets.

No, not them. The big one was that night at Upton Park. It was that night that Eric, for the first time since he had come back, Lazarus-like, from the longest ban in contemporary British football, was faced with a nasty rumpus. And, instead of getting shirty and swatting at an opposing player as an angry boy might at a fly, he acted with patience and calm, stepping in as the mediator. It was then that the true future was mapped out. It was that night it became clear Eric Cantona had decided to become the most important player ever to wear the red of Manchester United.

The path to that night began in May 1992, when Leeds thought they had got one over on United, their most hated rivals, as they snatched the title off the reds at the wire. But they were wrong. Six months after they had paraded through the streets of the city with the championship trophy, United pinched a much more momentous prize off them. And what's more, Leeds virtually gave Eric Cantona away. Cantona had been bought late in Leeds's championship campaign and – the opposite of Rodney Marsh at Manchester City in 1973 or Faustino Asprilla at Newcastle in 1996 – his unorthodox brilliance had helped them win it. He had added the extra sparkle to the team, there for all to see when he scored a hat-trick in the Charity Shield against Liverpool the following August.

But Leeds's manager, Howard Wilkinson, wasn't convinced. Appropriately nicknamed Sergeant Wilko, Wilkinson takes the military approach to football. He believes a collective effort can have no room for a maverick; members of the team must do what its leader tells them to do. Wilkinson was suspicious of Cantona, and thought him more interested in his own legend than the good of the team. He was worried that the fans adored the player so much it might prove upsetting for the others in the dressing-room. Sure, there was plenty of skill, like the time Cantona flicked the ball over a Chelsea defender's head and then volleyed it into the back of the net before it had landed on the other side. But the boss found Cantona so arrogant, so cocksure, so uncooperative to his tactical ideas of hit and hope that he lost patience. And boy could he sulk. When Wilkinson dropped him in favour of some player of more modest, but more malleable, skill, all the Frenchman could do was moan.

'He said he didn't mind who was in the team as long as he was,' Wilkinson snorted. Preposterous. Obviously they were right in France, he conjectured; after all, Cantona had fallen out with six clubs over there, been banned from the game on several occasions, even called the national team manager a bag of shite. One French official said wherever he went, Cantona left a trail of sulphur. Better to get a few bob for him before everyone else recognises the uncontrollable scale of his ego.

So when he got on the phone to Manchester United inquiring about Dennis Irwin and Alex Ferguson said he wasn't for sale, but was Cantona available, Howard Wilkinson honestly thought he'd off-loaded a liability. Still, he's not the only one to kick destiny out the window: someone turned the Beatles down once, too.

Cantona came to United at the same age George Best walked out at: at 26 Best was satisfied he had achieved everything; Cantona knew he hadn't even started. He cost just over £1 million – worth the money just to see the look on the face of the Leeds entrepreneur who showed the local television news the warehouse full of white 'Ooh Aah Cantona' T-shirts he had just had printed. His first appearance for the reds was as substitute for Ryan Giggs against Manchester City on 5 December 1992. With just one cross-field pass into Mark Hughes's feet, Alex Ferguson liked what he saw. A week later, Cantona made his full debut at home to Norwich. The team that day was: Schmeichel, Parker, Irwin, Bruce, Sharpe, Pallister, Cantona, Ince, McClair, Hughes, Giggs; the score was 1–0; Mark Hughes ('Youzeh') got the goal and the crowd, huddled into three sides as the Stretford End was redeveloped, was 34,500. Cantona scored his first goal for the club the following week at Chelsea and then scored in the next four games.

But not only did he score, thus solving United's temporary goal drought, he moved into space and he passed and helped team-mates to start scoring again as well. Two other players in the dream team under discussion here had their game transformed playing alongside Cantona. Mark Hughes found himself with room to manoeuvre and a partner who understood what he was up to. Ryan Giggs reckoned Cantona could judge exactly how fast a full-back could run, and paced his passes out to the wing accordingly. And the man himself loved the way Giggs and Hughes (and Kanchelskis and Ince and McClair) responded to his efforts. At last here were team-mates who could do something with his vision, who relished his eye, couldn't get enough of his skill. It made a change from Leeds.

Better than that, at Old Trafford Eric Cantona discovered not just a magnificent stadium, not just a team of incredibly high potential, not just a crowd as appreciative as they had been at Elland Road, but also a manager perfectly able to accommodate him and his extravagant self-will. Since Alex Ferguson had long since subsumed his own ego into the fabric of Old Trafford, he was not remotely threatened by Cantona's celebrity. He could be as big as he liked as long as he did the business on the field for Manchester United, because that was all Ferguson was interested in.

What Ferguson liked about Cantona is that he understood. Whatever his drawbacks – arrogance, intolerance, madness – Eric knew all about the cause: it had been him against the world since he was a youth in Auxerre and had taken out seven players from the opposition single-handedly in a car park after a game. Howard Wilkinson completely misread him. Cantona is not a dilettante, he's a worker. He is not a Gazza, he's self-disciplined. He takes his football almost as seriously as he takes himself. His authority problems were not of the Bestie, Paul McGrath, oh-bugger-it-I-can't-be-bothered-this-morning variety. First on, last off the training field, that's Eric. No, his problems came because he cared too much, hated losing, was wound up by injustice. For Fergie, that was the perfect pro.

In his first season for United, Cantona played 24 games and scored nine goals as United won the title. It is easy to say it now – United won the title: see, easy – but that year was the first time in 26 seasons they had done it. Cantona's contribution was immense. Not only did he score, and prompt and pass, he showed none of the nerves which had debilitated other expensive imports to Old Trafford. He came to the place infected with an arrogance that proved contagious, spreading through the dressing-room, filling his colleagues – whose will had crumpled the previous season – with certainty, with self-assurance, turning a bunch adept at falling at the final hurdle into a team of ruthless winners. In a dressing-room where the incomparable Mark Hughes was known as 'The Ledge' (short for legend) Cantona was dubbed 'Double Ledge'.

The fans loved him for that, the fact that he was different and knew himself to be better than the rest as an embodiment of their own sense of worth. This is what Richard Kurt, Cantona's Boswell, says of him: 'To reword Sherlock Holmes: with Eric, you must remove everything that is predictable or normal – whatever is left, however incredible or seemingly impossible, is what Eric will do.'

A whole hymnal of songs of praise to Cantona began to be heard, mostly penned by Peter Boyle, the poet laureate of K Stand. Boyle's biggest hit was a reworking of The Scaffold's 'Lily The Pink' called 'Eric The King', a song originally hijacked to sing the praises of Denis Law, the first monarch of Old Trafford:

We'll drink a drink a drink to
Eric the King, the King, the King
He's the leader of our football team
He's the greatest French footballer
That the world has ever seen.

and so on across eight verses.

When I asked Law, when I met him once, what he felt about Cantona now wearing his crown, he said: 'I can't think of anyone I'd rather.'

The following year, Manchester United fans were treated to the full range of Eric Cantona. He scored 18 league goals in 34 appearances, and six in the other competitions. His touch was at times sublime: a goal against Wimbledon in the FA Cup was particularly heavenly. In the midst of the Crazy Gang harum-scarum, he found himself on the edge of the area, with a high clearance zinging in his direction. He adjusted his position, carefully took the ball on his thigh, killing all its pace as he did so, then rolled it down towards his foot and sent it, banana-ing as it went, from 30 yards out, into the top left-hand corner of the goal. By the time the ball was in the net, the nearest Wimbledon defender had just arrived at his side.

There used to be an Australian children's television drama screened in Britain when I was a kid called *The Magic Boomerang*. In it our hero, a nine-year-old Aussie, had a boomerang which, when flung in the air, made time stand still. The boy would use its gifts to stop time while he dragged a baby from under the wheels of an on-rushing juggernaut, or pulled his dad from a truck about to topple over the edge of a gully. Well, Eric Cantona played as if in possession of that boomerang. Time seemed to stop around him, as he positioned himself in the mêlée and addressed the ball with all the time and precision of Stephen Hendry lining up the pink. Watching him in action there was a certainty about his movements, as if he knew, because he operated on a different level of physics from those around him, what was going to happen. Here is a statistic that proves the point: until the end of the 1996 season, Cantona had taken 15 penalties for United and scored with every one. He sent the keeper the wrong way with 14 of them.

There was another aspect of Cantona we saw in that year, too: as Ian Ridley, his biographer put it, the black as well as the red. He was sent off three times. At Galatasaray in the European Cup, he did little more than be sarcastic to the ref after the final whistle had blown, a crime for which he was punished with a four-match ban.

But at Swindon, in March, he lost all sight of proportion. We had seen Eric lose his temper in United's colours before, usually against Norwich. For some reason he took exception to John Polston; first flying in with a late two-footer at Old Trafford, then, at Carrow Road in the FA Cup, giving him a deft little back flick on the shoulder with his studs. The ref didn't notice either. But at Swindon the ref couldn't miss it: when Eric stamped all over John Moncur, another player not, you would have thought, the type to get worked up about, the look on the official's face was a picture. He was open-mouthed with astonishment that something so blatant should occur right under his nose. It was a look we were to see again, writ large.

Five days later Cantona was sent off at Arsenal. Unlucky this time, he did no more than collide with Tony Adams, but his escapade gave the press an unmissable opportunity to cast him as a villain. 'He's a nutter' was *The Sun*'s headline. The pundits foamed at the mouth. It was commercial joy for the papers. There has long been an English thirst – stretching back to the days when the Roundheads took a swipe at King Charles's expensively tailored collar – for seeing arrogance brought down a peg or two, cut down to size. And the papers were happy to quench that thirst.

'We're like Christmas every day for youse guys,' Alex Ferguson once complained at a press conference. He was right. When United played well, journalists could drool and sell hundreds of copies to the Red Army ('Cantona the conductor of United cantata' was *The Independent*'s headline after a glorious display against Sheffield Wednesday). And when one of the players was naughty, they could come over all self-righteous and sell to the equally sizeable – and ever-growing – army of United haters.

But there was something even better about Cantona for some parts of the press. At a time when the two political parties were adopting increasingly similar policies, there was one area in which there was a clear distinction: Europe. Labour was passionately pro the EC; the Tories passionately divided. The Tory press barons reckoned that by promoting a virulently anti-European line ('Up yours, Delors') they might, when election time came, turn public opinion against Labour and thus save the most unpopular government in the history of unpopular governments. So Eric was a godsend: talented, all right, but flawed and, even better, French. Not your straightforward, wholehearted British pro who goes in hard but fair – your Vinny Jones for instance – but your sneaky European, full of snide kicks and underhand back heels. See, that's what happens when you let those Europeans into this country, they stamp all over you.

After his indiscretions, the pursuit of Cantona was more appropriate to a mass murderer or philandering cabinet minister than a footballer sent off twice in five days: page after page, day after day. *The Sun*, by no coincidence the most rabidly anti-European paper, led the way. John Sadler, its sports columnist, set the tone, his words chosen with care and deliberation. Cantona should be deported, he demanded, now. A *Sun* reader was later to suggest to Eric that he 'fuck off back to France'. Same sentiment, different vocabulary.

The game Cantona returned from his unexpected mid-season break – a five-match suspension – we saw the red side again: he scored twice to win the Manchester derby. In the FA Cup final a few weeks later, he demonstrated that he was a man operating above nerves as he stroked two penalties away to complete United's double, this despite little Dennis Wise buzzing round him like an irritating mosquito, trying to upset his stride. Cantona's celebrity was now established: the Gallic genius, full of mysterious French fire, a player capable of making a difference at the highest level, the player who delivered the double. His peers knew what he was: he was voted PFA Player of the Year. Even John Moncur voted for him. Well, there really was no alternative.

His reputation as the most famous footballer in Britain was assured. And more than just a footballer. Exotic, unfathomable, deep: it was an image brilliantly honed by his boot sponsor Nike. Aware that he did not like doing anything at which he was not good, and was particularly not keen on speaking English to large audiences via cameras, the company encouraged him to restrict his public utterances to their campaigns. Thus he became the first sportsman in Britain to be scripted entirely by an advertising agency copy-writer. Cunningly, Nike played on his disciplinary problems, presenting them as evidence of a lack of convention which they liked to think mirrored their own corporate identity and which they hoped would help them sell trainers to the young and impressionable.

Meanwhile, we had no idea what Cantona was really like. Alex Ferguson told us he was quiet, undemonstrative, a family man who liked to sit on his own and read a book on the team's travels. But we saw none of that. We thought he came in black and white, moody, talking bollocks, improbably cool.

Cantona began the defence of the double in 1994–95 appropriately enough: he was sent off in a pre-season friendly against Glasgow Rangers. He went in late, two footed, all studs up, against a Rangers defender and was walking before the ref had got his card out. There was, said Alex Ferguson, defending his men as always, nothing malicious in it. 'The lad can't tackle,' Fergie said. 'Time and again I've told him, don't bother because you can't do it.' Ferguson's analysis was not entirely flannel. Cantona couldn't tackle. And, overcompensating, he tried too hard, sliding in late, with an intense look on his face, generally misinterpreted as malice.

Missing the first few games of the season through another suspension, banned, too, from Europe, Cantona had a stuttering start to the year. But he was just getting into his stride (12 goals in 21 games) when, in January 1995, stunning news broke. Alex Ferguson had bought Andy Cole, the Newcastle United goal machine, for a record £7 million. Unless you were a red it seemed almost unfair: Cole, at the time the most rapacious finisher in Britain, linking up with Cantona, the best player. It shouldn't be allowed. The first time they played together, Blackburn, then leading the table, were beaten at Old Trafford; Cole huffed and puffed, Cantona got the winner and kissed his shirt in celebration. Here we go again, you thought, the title is ours.

On the night of 25 January 1995, my mate Nigel and I were in the United section at Selhurst Park, just opposite the tunnel in one corner through which the players lope out from the dressing-rooms. We were there to see Cole and, more importantly, to see three more points on the march to the title. But, from the off, it didn't look like we were going to see much of either. It was a bad game, a bad pitch, a bad night. Cole had not yet adjusted his timing; he had a habit of jumping too early for every header, he seemed frustrated, he looked – it must have been the pressure of the transfer, we thought at the time – crap. And Eric, who had been magnificent against Blackburn, just looked pissed off, grumpy, irritated beyond reason that he was being man-marked efficiently by Richard Shaw, someone he evidently considered beneath him. Early in the second half he took a swing at Shaw in the centre circle. 'Aye, aye,' said Nigel, 'it's one of those nights.'

I didn't have time to reply before Eric had kicked Shaw's shin, and the Palace man had gone down, like a tower block under dynamite. The ref had missed the punch, but not the kick. Eric was off. He looked for a moment, in the inevitable push and shove, like a little boy, hurt, as if he was going to burst into tears. But as the referee indicated the direction to the dressing-room, he recovered his dignity, lifted the collar of his shirt, puffed out his chest and started to walk towards the bench. But Alex Ferguson, his mentor, like a father crossed once too often, refused to catch his eye. He was on his own this time. So he turned and walked towards the tunnel opposite us on his own.

We were there that night, but we didn't need to be. The cameras had the same view as us, clean, uninterrupted straight across the pitch. The pictures they got were corkers, enabling the scene to be replayed endlessly on the television, repeated time and again in newspapers. It became the most familiar sequence in British sporting history: Cantona walking off, stopping, turning to look at someone yelling obscenities at him, a woman laughing alongside. The athletic manner in which he vaulted the barrier, the way a man in a black leather jacket went down under the force of his Nikes, the look of shock – open-mouthed, eyebrows raised – on the faces in Palace's family stand behind. Eric being led off by Peter Schmeichel, the handbags that followed, Paul Ince jumping in.

And Nigel said to me: 'That's it, he's done it this time.' And we went home on the train feeling bereaved. Not sorry for him, but sorry for ourselves, left to face life without him, because this time he really had done it.

Oh, and David May got United's goal.

The headline on the front page of *The Sun* on Friday, 27 January 1995 was 'I'll Never Forget His Evil Eyes'. Below it was a panel: 'The Shame of Cantona; Full Story Pages 2, 3, 4, 5, 6, 22, 43, 44, 45, 46, 47, & 48'. On page 46, under the headline 'John Sadler on the Curse of Cantona', the pundit wrote: 'We have seen the best of him. Now we have got to see the back of him.'

From merely a famous French footballer, that kick elevated Cantona into the most celebrated sportsman this county has ever seen. For a week nobody, anywhere, talked about anything else other than his kung-fu assault. The media was full of it: Roy Hattersley said it was the most disgraceful thing that had ever happened at a British football ground (the families of the Hillsborough victims probably didn't agree), Brian Clough gave his sane and sober view that Cantona should be castrated. Not everyone agreed: Pat Crerand was on the radio more frequently than Chris Evans, seeking a little perspective. And my mum, at Sunday lunch, spoke for Middle England when she told me it was about time someone gave a mouthy yob a clip round the ear.

For Cantona, the season was over. First United banned him till the end of the term, then FIFA banned him world-wide, then the blazerati at the FA weighed in, extending the ban until October. Then the magistrates at Croydon gave him two weeks, a sentence commuted to community service. Without him United stuttered to a runners-up double.

It was a bad summer that followed. In August Cantona put in a transfer request after the FA said his appearance in a behind-closed-doors training session constituted a breach of his world-wide ban. *The Daily Mirror*, under the headline 'I Quit', announced he was off to join Internazionale. As was standard, we heard nothing from the man himself, but in probably the only instance of a quotable comment coming from a footballer's grandmother, Lucienne Cantona said: 'He does everything with his heart and at the moment his heart is hurting.'

Alex Ferguson flew to Paris to persuade 'mon genius', as he called him, to stay. He needed him: he'd just sold Ince, Hughes and Kanchelskis. He reminded Cantona how much he loved football in England, loved the crowds, the passion, the fact that the defenders couldn't man-mark a paper bag. Eventually, after six hours, a couple of Dover sole and a bottle of Chardonnay, Eric agreed he wanted more of it. So instead of going, he waited, and trained and was patient. And he spent a lot of time thinking.

On 1 October 1995, after an absence of 248 days, he returned to an exultant Old Trafford. 'He's been punished for his mistakes,' read the accompanying announcement from his publicity manipulators at Nike. 'Now it's someone else's turn.'

That day it was Liverpool's. He supplied a cross for Nicky Butt to score the first goal within two minutes, and later, inevitably, he scored himself from a penalty, which he celebrated by spinning around the goal stanchion. The next day every headline in every paper was about him, which was a touch unfair on Robbie Fowler, who got a sparkling pair. But then Robbie Fowler, he's not exactly Eric Cantona. In among the celebrations, siren voices were heard. The real test was yet to come, the cassandras wailed. Away from the cosy hero-worship of Old Trafford, at Leeds or Anfield or West Ham, where the yobs lurk, then we'll see the provocation. And then Eric would blow up. Always had done, always will. It was just a matter of time.

In a sense, they were right. What everyone recognised about Eric Cantona was that he played without fear. He did things with a football that other players would not attempt, whether through fear of failure, fear of ridicule, or fear of the manager's ire. If his efforts failed, he shrugged his shoulders and tried again. When they succeeded, his touches and goals, passes and back flicks gave United another dimension.

But just as he was fearless with the ball, so he was when he retaliated against those he thought had wronged him. He was fearless of reputation or consequence. Time and again, in France and England, he stamped on wrong-doers and was sent off. It didn't matter how many times he was suspended or for how long, nothing would be in his mind the next time he felt he was wronged, except the need to dispense instant justice: Eric justice.

On the night of the Selhurst disaster, as he walked from the pitch, sent off for once more retaliating against perceived wrongs, he was confronted by a prat mouthing his ignorance two feet from his chin. Faced with that, Cantona did what most of us would love to do, he smacked him. But most of us wouldn't behave like that because of fear: fear the guy might hit us back, fear of arrest, fear, were we professional footballers with our contracts up for renewal, that the chairman, sitting in the stands, might not take too kindly to this sort of thing. A certain self-preservation might tell us not to leap feet-first over a three-foot-high fence. Cantona has none of that.

And this was the central tension of the man. This bravery, this absolute indifference to consequence, the things that made him a great player, also made him temperamentally unsuited to a game which, by its very nature, requires strict adherence to the rules. As the would-be philosopher himself once put it: 'I play with passion and fire. I have to accept that sometimes the fire does harm. But I cannot be what I am without these other sides to my character.'

The problem was the principal sufferers of harm were United, the club he had grown to love. When he missed five games through suspension in the 1993–94 season, the reds lost three and stumbled, fortuitously, through an FA Cup semi-final against Oldham. He was banned from the first four matches in the Champions League in 1994, and by the time he came back, it was too late. And then he missed the second half of the 1994–95 season, when his team-mates, never close to the heights they had scaled the previous year, scrapped their way to the runners-up double. He was the player who made the difference; but he could only make the difference if he was playing.

Every game we were waiting, for a defender to push him too far, for niggle to turn to violence. This was a talent we had on a short lease, we knew, not freehold. And the next time he exploded – stupidly, recklessly, gloriously – the lease would expire. Even Alex Ferguson couldn't tolerate another indiscretion.

Which was what was so important about that night in Upton Park. He didn't lose it. Nor did he subsequently during the rest of the 1995–96 season. Cantona, in his long period of exile and self-assessment, seemed to recognise that he had to control the red mists he thought were vital to his spirit. He once assumed he couldn't have one without the other. Now he realised that if he didn't check his temper, he would be separated from the thing he loved: football.

As his temper stayed under wraps, a debate raged in the papers over whether he was the same player. Many thought he wasn't. They were right, he wasn't. But it wasn't as they imagined: he was better. In later stages of 1995–96, he just got better and better.

To put what Cantona did that season into perspective, it is important to remember where United were in October 1995. Ince, Kanchelskis and Hughes had all gone; Steve Bruce was creaking and Gary Pallister full of injury. In short, the core of the great 1993–94 double-winning side had gone, replaced, as Richard Kurt nicely put it, by an 'overdose of youthful callow'. Cantona gradually instilled a belief in them. The squad of young players – Giggs, Scholes, Butt, Beckham, the Nevilles – were used to winning together, they had grown in victory. Cantona merely encouraged them to believe they could continue the habit at the higher level. He showed them what training was about, what pride in your work and achievement was about; he took the captain's arm-band and with it the responsibility. Particularly in front of goal – 13 games in 1995–96 were decided by Cantona winners or equalisers. Against Sunderland in the FA Cup third round he equalised on 80 minutes; against QPR at Loftus Road he equalised on 90 minutes;

against Arsenal, Spurs, Coventry, Newcastle and West Ham in the league he got the only goal of the game. Where the previous year without him United had stumbled at the last, this year with him they reined in the most dangerous rivals they had faced in the '90s – Newcastle – and won the league with real panache. He had now removed all doubt. He was truly great.

Some people, though, remained unconvinced. In the week before the FA Cup final it was announced that Eric Cantona had been voted the football writers' Footballer of the Year. At the offices of *The Sun* John Sadler and Brian Woolnough, football correspondent, were fuming. It was a disgrace, they fulminated, that a man who had done what Cantona had done should be thus rewarded, their colleagues should be ashamed of themselves. Because they, Brian and John, wouldn't forget Selhurst, couldn't forgive the man. The lack of generosity in their memories came as no surprise to their readers as they seem incapable of reporting any match involving England and Germany without reference to events that occurred more than 50 years ago.

When Cantona received his prize at the awards dinner, I found myself at the table next to *The Sun's*. And after Eric gave his magnanimous speech and everyone stood to applaud the greatest player of his and many other generation, Sadler and Woolnough sat in their seats, resolutely refusing to clap, full of pique. How, three days later, at the FA Cup final, they must have looked back at their petty gesture and squirmed.

If there was any thought that United would relax in the 1996 Cup final, and open out since they had already won the league the week before, it was to underestimate how anxious Alex Ferguson was to take his place in history as the first manager to achieve the double double. United strung five across the middle and waited for Liverpool to make the first move. They didn't: Liverpool were scandalous, bankrupt of ideas and enterprise, as if all their effort had been expended on the selection of their big match suits.

In the stands, United's fans relaxed, though, partying throughout, outsinging their Scouse chums by a Mersey tunnel of a margin. Most of their praises were directed at Cantona: tricolours with his face printed on flew everywhere in the United end, the 'Marseillaise' was sung to distraction, three worshippers sitting near me were decked in full French national costume, stripy Breton jumpers and berets and had strings of real onions around their necks where football fans usually drape scarves.

Cantona didn't let them down. In the 80th minute of this dreary farrago of misplaced passes and scuffed shots, United won a corner. Beckham took it. It looped toward the penalty spot, and David James, until then indomitable but choosing this moment to make his customary one mistake per match, mispunched. The ball dropped towards Cantona, lurking just inside the area. Up went the boomerang. Time stopped as he shifted his weight, twisting his spine like someone in the clutches of a sadistic osteopath, getting himself in the right place for when the ball finally arrived. When it did, he hit it, cleaner than anything had been hit all afternoon, back from whence it came, through six Liverpool defenders into the one unguarded square foot of the net. When he realised what he had done, Cantona ran, face split in triumph, towards his fans, lifting his shirt up at them as if to show them who he played for. When his colleagues caught up with him – first Beckham, then Irwin, lastly Schmeichel, belting from the back – they formed an adoring, grateful huddle round him, each player roaring their thanks into his face.

At that point they knew, we knew, you suspect even John Sadler of *The Sun* knew, even if it goes wrong some time in the future, Eric Cantona had given us something rare. He had given us the sight of greatness.

THE BOSS

Alex Ferguson. Life began: 7.11.86

What everyone at Manchester United says about Alex Ferguson is that he likes to be involved in every aspect of the club, he likes to know what's going on, what the groundsman's doing about that bobble just outside the 18-yard box, which 11-year-old in the Durham School of Excellence has a tidy left foot and who's drinking where, on what night and with whom. He likes to be in charge.

'Listen, at this club you get sleepless nights if you play badly in the reserves,' Les Sealey, United's erstwhile second string goalie said when he was there. 'Honest, there's always someone watching you, and if you slack, word will get back. To him.'

One day in the spring of 1996, when we were filming *The Manchester United Family Tree*, we got a hint of his omnipresence, of the tentacles Fergie spreads across the biggest club in Britain. I had had this idea that it would be good to talk to someone who had failed at Old Trafford, to get them to tell us what the pressure to succeed was like and what happened when you could not live up to all the expectations. I suggested we start at the bottom: with Ralph Milne.

When you look at the United team today, with class in every position, studded with internationals, chocker with the brightest young players (and that's just the reserves), it is easy to see that Ralph Milne should only have been allowed inside Old Trafford if he had paid his money at the turnstile like everyone else. But even in those dark, dismal, transitional days of 1989 when Mal Donaghy was at the crux of the side, when the best you hoped for from a season was

171

39 mediocre games and a victory over Liverpool, we in the stands knew that Ralphie was ostensibly not a United player. Bought from Bristol City in 1988 to replace Jesper Olsen, Milne cost £175,000 (roughly £170,000 more than he was worth). Full-backs were not, in this winger's scheme of things, people to be tantalised, toyed with, destroyed; they were there to be avoided. He beat fewer people in his time on the Old Trafford flanks than even Mickey Thomas, who – I have a vague recollection – once beat a bloke. Milne was pilloried mercilessly by the critics on the United Road, hammered for his lack of presence, held up as evidence in the stands that Fergie didn't know what he was doing (how wrong we all turned out to be). You should have felt sorry for Milne. You would have done, if you didn't despise him.

We got his number from Norman Whiteside. If anyone could use the 100 quid interview fee, Norm reckoned, Ralphie could. So Steve, the assistant producer, contacted him, sounded him out on the phone, conducted a sort of casting session and said we'd get back to him if we wanted to include him in the show. Not a good television performer, was Steve's prognosis after he had replaced the receiver. Nervous, he thought, probably wouldn't add anything to the programme. Much like his form as a player, then. Sam, the director, decided it wasn't an avenue he wanted to explore anyway, so Steve rang back to tell Ralph we wouldn't be needing him after all. Mrs Milne answered the phone. Ralph was out, she said, and anyway, if that was the BBC, he didn't want to be interviewed. Fair enough, thought Steve, saved me a job.

The next morning we were due to film at the Cliff, taking in shots of the boys training, then interviewing Steve Bruce and Ryan Giggs. When we arrived, had found a space among the gleaming pieces of German mechanical engineering littering the car park, and were starting to unload the equipment, Fergie caught sight of us. He angrily beckoned Sam over, the rest of us realised from his demeanour it was best to stand our distance.

Cheeks purpling up, eyes narrowed, mouth about three millimetres from Sam's nose, finger stabbing towards his chest, Fergie looked concerned. 'I was reluctant to be involved in your programme but the chairman persuaded me,' he said to Sam. 'Because he said you were going to do a positive film on us, not the usual stitch up.'

'We are. We've got no intention of stitching anybody up,' said Sam, which was true. 'We're just doing a fun, anecdotal history of the club.'

'Is that so?' said Fergie, bristling. 'So why did you contact Ralphie Milne?'

And we all thought, as Sam reported the incident back to us, how the hell did he know?

There have been five managers at Manchester United since Sir Matt Busby retired. Wilf McGuinness, who couldn't cope and lost his hair through the pressure of it all. Frank O'Farrell, who couldn't cope and went to live in Torquay. Tommy Docherty, who could cope, won the FA Cup, built an extravagant team, but was ultimately laid low as much by the enemies he accrued along the way as by his own stupidity. Dave Sexton, who would have been able to cope at most other clubs, but was so shy he found the media attention at United intolerable ('how I ever became a coach, I'll never know,' he told me, 'standing up in front of people, spouting'). Ron Atkinson, who loved the attention, won two FA Cups, but fell to the pressure of expectation (that and the fact his last five signings – Peter Barnes, Terry Gibson, Mark Higgins, John Sivebaek and Colin Gibson – were in the Ralphie Milne class). And now there is Alex Ferguson.

Here's a little test for United fans. Who would you prefer to be in charge of your club: a lovely old softie, whom non-United fans across the country have taken to their heart, always ready with a gag for the press, and invariably sweet to camera crews visiting his training ground? Or a control freak, displaying symptoms of advanced paranoia and possessing a siege mentality so entrenched he would be welcomed with open arms as a negotiator for the Ulster Unionist Party? One other thing to help you make the choice. The first bloke has never won anything. And the second, in the last ten years, has won the following: three League titles, three FA Cups, two doubles, one League Cup and one European Cup Winners' Cup.

The point about Alex Ferguson is that those very characteristics which appear to make him unattractive, the ones which make fans of other clubs spit at the mere mention of his name – toughness, lack of compromise, a hatred of losing so profound that it can manifest itself as a persecution complex – are the ones which make him a brilliant manager of Manchester United. As his duel with Kevin Keegan in the spring of 1996 proved, in football, as in life, nice blokes come second.

Except with Ferguson, more than anyone else you could come across, that surface we see as he conducts his daily business is deceptive. There are sides to him few outside his immediate work circle ever get to witness. Peter Davenport, for instance, told me that the morning of the 1992 FA Cup final, when he was about to play for Sunderland against Liverpool, he was sitting in his hotel room and the phone rang.

'So I answered it,' says Dav. 'And this voice goes: "Hi, it's Alec, I'm just ringing to wish you luck, son." And, though I sort of recognised the voice, I said: "Alec who?" And the voice goes: "Alec Ferguson." I couldn't believe it – two years after he'd transferred me, a week after United had just blown the league to Leeds, he took the time and trouble to ring me up. It was incredible.'

And Ian Ridley, *The Independent on Sunday*'s astute football correspondent, remembers how he was invited by Fergie after a game into one of the several suites he keeps at Old Trafford for personal entertaining. Once up there, in the company of a couple of other trusted hacks and friends, the Boss opened a bottle of malt and started to talk. Ridley, the new boy, just thought it best to sit in the corner and listen, observe. He was astonished by the man who emerged from within: warm, relaxed, considerate, dewy-eyed with nostalgia, a man in love with his profession. In short, the perfect host.

Now most of us, since our principal goal in life is that other people should like us, would want the world to know we were, underneath it all, sweethearts, warm, thoughtful human beings who love nothing more than a natter about football over a bottle of Laphroaig. We would take whatever opportunity came our way to make sure people knew that. Politicians employ spin doctors to do this for them. Pop stars retain press agents. Wannabes and neverwillbes recruit Max Clifford. As manager of Manchester United there are plenty of opportunities, a boundless ocean of media outlets, on which to float a benevolent public image. Tommy Docherty relished that, he kept a cuttings file the size of a coffin about himself, and fooled us on the terraces for five years at Old Trafford as to his real self. Ron Atkinson relished it too, particularly if the media were prepared to stump up a bob or two for his jolly wisecracks. Fergie appears not to care less that the wider world has little inkling of the real man. As far as he is concerned it's irrelevant. No, more than that. It's a distraction from the important job in hand, the one-track course on which he has set himself: total world football domination.

'He sees football as a cause,' says Mark McGhee, now manager of Wolves but once a player under Ferguson at Aberdeen. 'A cause to which he expects you to give 100 per cent. Everything else is secondary. And I mean everything else. He only wants people around him who are prepared to accept the challenge, as he calls it. To take on the cause.'

The cause?

'His cause: to prove everybody wrong.'

And Ferguson appears to be prepared to do anything, even diminish his own self, to achieve it. If making himself unpopular will help develop a winning attitude at the club, who cares? He doesn't.

So remind me again: who do you want as manager of your football team?

Ferguson has been living the cause all his life. Forged in the protestant work ethic of the shipyards of Govan, he became what was considered the apex of achievement in Loyalist Glasgow, a Rangers player. He didn't have much in the way of talent, but at least he knew it and knew how to recognise it in others. I remember seeing him in the bar after a European Cup tie in Budapest, wrapping his arm around Denis Law's shoulders and saying: 'Here we are, two great Scottish centre-forwards together. You've got 65 caps and I've got fuck all.' But what he lacked in talent he made up for in energy, vigour, aggression. Oh, all right, he was a filthy bugger, sent off as often for Rangers as Eric Cantona has been for Manchester United.

The fire, whatever it was that drove him, wasn't satisfied simply by being a Rangers player and stamping on fenian shins four times a season, however. Nor was the thought of spending his retirement behind the bar at the pub he owned telling folk he used to be somebody, an idea that appealed. Instead, when he hung up his boots, he became what most of his playing career – telling referees what they should be doing, pointing out deficiencies to colleagues and opponents alike, moaning about the press – had been a rehearsal for. He became a manager.

At East Stirling, he tore into the job with frightening zeal. Contemporaries remember him at the club all hours, obsessed with the idea of making them something, terrifying performances out of his charges by the sheer force of his will. So much so that he was aghast when his mad whirl of commitment was not matched by the fans. Apathy: he couldn't work that one out, never has been able to. Why was no one coming to watch the games he'd worked so bloody hard to prepare for? So he strapped a loudspeaker to the roof of his car and toured the local housing estates in the manner of an aspirant politician, telling everyone to bloody well get off their backsides and come watch his team.

It was, though, at Aberdeen that he found a real vehicle for the cause. Never mind that he was Glaswegian, and proud of it. Now he was in exile on the north-east coast, he wanted all those bastards in the west to sit up and take note. He told his players there was only one thing that they had to do: break the smug Old Firm hegemony. Bust that and they'd be top dogs. Those Glaswegians, they're so arrogant they'll think it can't be done, they'll laugh at you for even trying. Prove every one of them wrong, that was his aim, and that was the challenge, as he calls it, he set the players.

In eight years he won ten trophies for Aberdeen, including the Cup Winners' Cup, and he discovered some great players – Willie Miller, Alex McLeish, Gordon Strachan. And was he a hard taskmaster? 'Oh aye,' remembers Mark McGhee. 'He put pressure on you to perform all the time and he expected you to have the mental strength to withstand it. If you repaid him, he was incredibly loyal to you. But if you didn't, he wasn't slow to tell you. He was very honest.'

In the end, though, life became a little easy for Alex Ferguson up in the Granite City. The interest was seeping out of the challenge. Mark McGhee says his team-talks became a little repetitive. All that 'we'll show those Glaswegians', it became a touch less effective after the Dons had been consistently better than them for eight years. 'I think I'd come to the end of the road,' Fergie admitted to me. 'You know, I was getting a little restless in the afternoons.'

Fortunate, then, that the biggest club in Britain, the one that in 1986 represented the biggest challenge in football (apart from Halifax Town, that is), the place that could fill his afternoons, offered an outlet for his energy. It was Bobby Charlton who recommended Ferguson to United. Charlton, by then a club director, never really reckoned Ron Atkinson was the man for the job, thought him not involved enough with the club, too concerned with cosying up to his first team and not paying enough heed to the youth operation, the great Busby inheritance. Besides, Charlton believed, Ron had taken a wrong turning. His players were for ever boozing, drink-driving, scrapping in training. No way was he ever going to win the title with such a slapdash bunch. Ferguson, Sir Bob had heard, liked his players to be focused, liked to know what was going on, liked to be in charge. Charlton told the board, when they started to panic that Ron's team were slipping towards the depths of the first division and showing little inclination to resurface, that the man for the job was Alex Ferguson.

According to Michael Crick in his excellent book *Manchester United: The Betrayal of a Legend*, Martin Edwards, a man who, in 1981, had sacked a previous manager (Dave Sexton) and then failed to land the replacement he wanted (Laurie McMenemy), insisted on a little insurance this time round. So Ferguson was sounded out and said he was interested days before Big Ron was sacked.

All this is obviously fiction, since it is against league rules to tap up another club's manager when you have one in place, and United would never do that. Besides, both Ferguson and Edwards have denied any contact was made until Big Ron was in his Merc heading south down the M6. Clearly it was just a matter of speedy negotiations that allowed Fergie to turn up to work at Old Trafford the day after Ron left. Evidently it was merely an example of efficient recruitment that allowed all the loose ends to be tied and contract negotiations to be complete in readiness for Fergie to face a dressing-room full of players who had not yet even had time to recover from Ron's farewell bevvy the night before.

So why did Fergie take the job? He was, after all, sitting pretty in Aberdeen and United were not only a mess, they were a mess that had inflated ideas about what their place in the football hierarchy should be: at the top. 'Poisoned chalice' was the standard job description in the press at that time for Manchester United manager.

'The tradition, the history, the romance of the place appealed,' he told me. 'You just want to be part of it.'

And how did he find it?

'He was in awe of the place when he first arrived,' Norman

Whiteside says. 'He kept coming up to me and Robbo in training and saying: "Big place this, big place."'

'He was,' according to Peter Davenport, 'very nervous. Like a kitten. I remember the first time he announced a team, he went through it and he said: "Right, we'll have Clayton, Remi and Kevin in midfield and up front we've got Frank, Peter and Nigel. Okay lads?" And there was a moment's pause, then Robbo said: "Nigel? Who's Nigel?" And Fergie points at me and goes: "Him, Nigel Davenport."'

Romance, awe, nerves. Not words you associate with Alex Ferguson at all. But then, we never get to see the real man. He didn't get off to a great start. The first team he picked – for an away game at Oxford United – was: Turner, Duxbury, Albiston, McGrath (Olsen), Moran, Hogg, Blackmore, Stapleton, Moses, Davenport, Barnes. In front of 13,545 the new man's side lost 2–0. Despite that, what was not in doubt from the off was that United got for their swift piece of business a man who, if he was going to fail, would not fail for lack of effort, passion or – another favourite Fergie word – commitment.

It was a commitment gap that led to Fergie's problems in his first few years at Old Trafford. Players like Moran, McGrath, Whiteside and Strachan dominated the team he inherited. They were strong players, skilful players, great players, but were also men who approached their profession with a sense of humour, a degree of proportion. Proportion and humour are not really characteristics you would attribute to Alex Ferguson at the best of times. And in 1986 he found nothing to amuse or divert him about the 19 years of underachievement he had inherited. 'The day I came here, the job was to win the league, make no mistake about it,' he told me. 'We couldn't accept Liverpool winning the league, or Arsenal who were now emerging. We couldn't let it happen; we couldn't tolerate it.'

There he was, in his office by 7.30 a.m. every day, restructuring the youth system, working on the reserves, training with the first team, negotiating with other managers, constantly scanning the teletext for hint of transfer-list action, scouting schools games in the afternoons, watching other teams in the evening, back home at midnight and poring over videos until two, three in the morning. And there was the star core of his team unable to train properly because they'd been out having a good time the previous night. In the red corner the Calvinist. In the blue, the swaggering socialite free-spirits, as he called them. The early clashes were noisy.

'The first thing Gordon did when he heard that Alec had been made manager was to shake everyone by the hand and say, "bye-bye, I'm out of here,"' remembers Peter Davenport.

'I gave the lads fair warning,' Strachan told me when I interviewed him for the *United Family Tree*. 'I told them what he was like at Aberdeen. But he was like a pussy cat for the first few weeks, three months even. They were all looking at me, cos I'd made him out to be Hannibal Lecter or something. Then we played Wimbledon away, and that afternoon they all looked at me again and you could see them thinking, "Yup, Gordon, I take your point."'

Wimbledon away, all those Crazy Gang welcomes, rock hard balls, salt in your half-time tea and freezing cold baths. 'Horrible pitch, horrible team, horrible,' is how Giggs sums the place up. The first time Ferguson took his team there, they didn't want to know, and lost. Afterwards, the Boss went apoplectic. The full-on temper was let loose, the legendary temper, the one which during his days at Aberdeen had seen him fling the kit skip all over the dressing-room, sending a jock-strap flying through the air to roost on a player's head. The story has it that this individual was too terrified to move to take it off, so just sat there with it dangling over his forehead as the storm crashed around him. Which was a mistake since when Ferguson caught sight of it he gave him an additional bollocking for daring to sit there during a bollocking wearing an athletic support on his head.

Now, on this occasion, the first sniff of the Fergie fury the United players had seen, with the half-time tea service performing a passable impression of the Red Arrows, Peter Barnes had been substituted with half an hour to go (about an hour too late in some opinions, but that's another matter) and Fergie looked everywhere to bring him into the exchange of views he was initiating in the dressing-room. But Barnes was nowhere to be seen. He wasn't in the showers, not in the lavs, nowhere. Eventually the hurricane dissipated and Fergie departed. And the moment he had gone, the door from the showers opened and a head appeared. 'It was Barnes,' remembers Strachan. 'He'd been hiding in the bath for half an hour, ducking under the freezing water whenever Fergie came looking for him and was by now blue with cold.'

Once switched on, the 'hair-dryer', as the players called it, because he stood so close to them when delivering his criticisms they got a blow wave thrown in with the bollocking, was in constant use in those early days. 'You used to try to make sure you weren't the man with the ball as half-time approached,' remembers Mark Hughes. 'He seemed always to pick on the last mistake before the whistle and explode at that person. It used to scare the living daylights out of us, but it was only because of the tremendous will to win that he had.'

The Mersey domination, the new Ferguson cause, however, was not to be broken by disturbed crockery alone. By the end of the 1988–89 season all he had to show for two years of toil and yelling was a runners-up slot to Liverpool when United had come so far behind they might as well have come 15th. That plus a growing propensity during post-match interviews to find anyone to blame – the ref, the opposition, Brian Barwick, the editor of *Match of the Day* and a life-long Liverpool fan – anyone, except his team or himself. Which was odd because in those early days, both seemed culpable: his team seemed to have no shape, no purpose, no direction and he had no apparent idea what to do about it. Nothing made sense. It was not as if he had shirked tough decisions. After the reds lost at home to Forest in the sixth round of the Cup in 1989 (thus preventing United meeting Liverpool in the semi, that terrible day at Hillsborough) he decided his team required not so much major surgery as an entire organ transplant. 'I said to myself you're going to have to build a team that is prepared to accept a few challenges,' he said of those times. 'Not just today and then they can't muster the energy to do it the next day.'

Typically, when the scalpel was wielded, he did not concern himself with personal popularity. Out went the hedonists, Strachan, McGrath and Whiteside, our favourites. And in came – heaven preserve us – Danny Wallace and Neil Webb (Pallister and Ince came too, but at first they looked useless as well).

Back in 1989 Fergie didn't seem to move so much in mysterious ways as bizarre ones. Hidden shallows, we thought. He told us to trust him, but by the autumn of that year, the lads on the terraces had turned on him. He claimed to have a master plan, but all we could see was a Scottish whinger with an inflated reputation for doing things in the small world north of the border. A man who'd got rid of all the talent and was leading us nowhere.

'Three years of excuses, tara Fergie' read the banner held up in the crowd to greet the third anniversary of his arrival at Old Trafford. By January 1990, after a run of eight games without a victory, United were fifth bottom and Ferguson was, it appeared from the outside, about to be seeking new employment. Few on the terraces would have shed a tear. An FA Cup third-round tie at Forest was cast as the make-or-break game.

'Troubled boss Ferguson, reconciled to trial by TV as another crisis grips Old Trafford' was *The Sun*'s headline on 8 January 1990, two days before the match. It topped a spread of features fulminating against his tenure at the club. Willie Morgan was particularly damning: 'Fergie's wasted £13 million on untried, inexperienced players like Gary Pallister who are not up to the job,' he wrote.

Unexpectedly, in that tabloid witch hunt, only Terry Gibson, rightly shown the door by Fergie at Old Trafford (the very low but wide door in the corner), showed any prescience. 'One thing's for sure, whoever takes over will be the luckiest boss in the land,' Gibson was quoted as saying in *The Sun*, as if the departure was already a done thing. 'How would you like to take over that group of players? There is so much talent that one day they will be a real force.' The headline on the back page that day, incidentally, was a familiar one: 'Stupid Gazza breaks arm.'

According to Sir Bobby Charlton, however, the board was not to be persuaded by press campaigns or fan pressure – which must have been a first. 'During that time we never, ever, discussed Alex Ferguson's position,' Sir Bobby maintains. 'Because we knew what he was doing was right.'

Short of Martin Edwards putting the minutes of the board meeting on display in the Old Trafford museum, we will never know whether Sir Bobby is indulging in generous dollops of post-rationalisation here or not. Because Mark Robins, stooping to connect with Mark Hughes's perfect through ball, won Fergie that game, the reds went on to win the Cup and from almost that goal the momentum was set. Thus if any United fan ever comes across Robins in a bar, he should buy him a very, very large drink. Because whatever might now be said, without Mark Robins, you don't have to be Mystic Meg to work out, Fergie would have gone. And then we wouldn't be where we are today.

So what was Fergie doing behind the scenes that was so right? I mean apart from turning up personally on Lynne Giggs's doorstep to persuade her to let her son sign for him rather than City; apart from buying Lee Sharpe for nothing and then protecting him when he had his difficulties; apart from improving the training so his team became the fittest in the land; apart from sorting out the press so that their demands didn't impinge on his work. ('The press were always coming round,' he told me. 'I said to them, there's no way I'm gonna be restricting my job giving you something every day. I said, give me a call, if there's something to tell you I will.') Apart from all those things, then, what was he doing that was so right?

What he was doing was casting the club in his own image. All institutions take their lead from the head. Virgin we understand as the gutsy underdog; slightly dippy, eccentric, a corporation we imagine with a beard and sweater, like its boss. The FA we conceive as bumbling, hopeless, amateur, a flab in a blazer. You know, Graham Kelly-like. At Manchester United everyone hates, abhors, detests and loathes one thing above all others. Losing.

I remember walking on to the plane the press and players shared after United were hammered by Barcelona. As we had to file our stories and wire back our pictures, the press party arrived at the airport about half an hour after the team had strapped on their seat belts. When we approached the steps to the plane, several of the scribes, no fans of Fergie or United, started to make jokes about not giggling. 'No laughing, lads,' said one senior broadsheet man. 'Fergie'll plant a Glasgow kiss on anyone caught sniggering within a quarter of a mile of the plane.'

What struck us, though, as we entered the body of the plane, would have wiped the smile off the most die-hard Scouser. The air was charged with silent, abject, absolute misery. We had to make our way through to the cheap seats at the back past Mark Hughes, in a neck brace, just gazing into space, Eric Cantona resolutely looking out of the window, Denis Irwin, staring straight through us, blank, shell-shocked. There was inevitably a hold-up as some representative of the great British sporting media failed to squeeze himself into a seat and I found myself standing in the aisle alongside a seated Fergie for a couple of difficult, embarrassing moments. What are you meant to say in those circumstances? 'Never mind, eh?' scarcely seemed adequate. I needn't have worried; conversation was not, he made it clear, on his agenda. He had turned his back towards the aisle, shoulders twisted, head down, no mean feat of dexterity in the confines of a charter plane, pretending to concentrate all his effort on pouring a glass of wine: an action which took him about ten minutes. He was unable, totally incapable, of meeting anyone's eye.

'Alec is a terrible loser. Terrible,' says Mark McGhee. 'Whether at cards, a trivia quiz, at football, it hurts him physically to lose. And he makes sure you know how much it hurts him.' As a fan, I love that – to know that the club is in the hands of someone who cares. You could see that the day they trooped off at West Ham after the last game of the 1995 season. They'd just lost the league title to Blackburn, but they looked as though they'd been relegated. Young lads, Scholes, Butt, Giggsy, people who might in other circumstances, at other clubs, have looked chuffed that they'd just come second, tramped to the dressing-room, black socks around their ankles, shin-guards flopping, looking as though they had just heard that their mother had a terminal illness. Alex Ferguson, looking at them, a picture of misery, would have thought that day, yes, that's my boys, they won't forget this, they won't let it happen again.

Though we hadn't worked it out at the time, back in 1989, what he was doing was planting the seed, sowing the crop he would harvest later.

What Ferguson did at United was identify a cause (better Liverpool) and then commit all his and his players efforts to it. It sounds simple, almost as simple as Matt Busby's apparently magical team-talks ('just go out and enjoy yourselves'), but the distractions open to Manchester United staff are many-fold. Ferguson's ruthless focus, and his Stalinistic capacity to ensure everyone thought he knew exactly what they were up to even if he didn't, ensured such distractions were kept on a short rein.

'I can't have my players out doing commercial things every day, out opening shops and doing charity things,' he told me. 'Energy is so vital with footballers, when you're playing cup finals every week out there. Someone needs to be in control of that. Someone *has* to be in control of that.'

By control, by sheer force of effort, Ferguson slowly made the whole disparate, amorphous enterprise point in the same direction.

What he deemed important was right, and anybody who disagreed found Old Trafford an uncomfortable place to be.

The problem with making the whole enterprise bend to your will is that sometimes your bad habits rub off with the good. In 1992, after he had won the FA Cup, the Cup Winners' Cup and the Rumbelows Cup, Ferguson looked set fair to deliver the one we all craved, the one which proved you really were better than your peers, the one the Scousers had apparently annexed: the championship. All was going well – or, if not well, then at least effectively – until the last. Then, in six games, we went from racing certainties to dead beats, from Ian Botham to Ray Illingworth, from Noel Gallagher to Mike Flowers. We lost at home to Forest, we drew at Luton, we lost away at West Ham, we lost, God help us, away at Liverpool. It was awful, that night at Upton Park, with chirpy cockney characters, already relegated, making out like they'd won the league. We handed the championship to (take a deep breath, a couple of Nurofen and go and lie down in a darkened room) Leeds.

But what was worse for the bar-room bore, it seemed our manager lost it for us. Dithering with team selection, leaving out Kanchelskis a week after he had scored the winner against Southampton ('Andrei is my match-winner,' he said after the game), leaving out Hughes against Forest when Nigel Clough was plugging an injury crisis playing at centre-back, going all defensive when we should have been attacking, confusing the team, communicating his nerves to the players. Remember him after the West Ham game, a picture of shattered nerves, whingeing about the Hammers' 'obscene' effort? The players must have thought, blimey, he's gone. They knew how much he cared – too much, perhaps – and they were terrified at his reaction should they fail. So terrified, in fact, they couldn't play any more.

'The modern media are so quick to blame the manager,' he said when I asked him if he was to blame for 1992 and all that. 'I can hand on heart say I was getting on to a few players about performance around the middle of the season. But in the latter part, definitely not. If anything I laid off them. We lost because we had a lot of things against us. Four games in six days, you can't counter that.'

But what about the tinkering? Didn't he disrupt their pattern and mind-set through nervous juggling of his team-sheet resources?

'No, there was some thought because the pitch was so bad out there I was caught in a dilemma of whether we should start playing long forward passes. We toyed with the idea for maybe a couple of games, then abandoned it. No, no, make no mistake about it, it was the run-in that did it.'

So it was another case of a gap between the explanation we sought from a distance, and the reality?

'Really, it was the run-in, you can't legislate for that.'

Interestingly the players agree it was not the boss's fault. Steve Bruce admits the team went out for those last few games thinking they were going to lose, but blames himself and his mates for that; he claims Fergie did his best to calm them. And Mark Hughes concurs. 'I don't remember him being nervous,' Hughes recalls. 'I think he thought we were very nervous. I remember him hiring a comedian for the pre-match meal before the Liverpool game to try and relax us. I felt sorry for the guy, we weren't exactly in the mood to laugh at his gags.' Only Bryan Robson seemed to enjoy the comedian's act. But then the bloke's party piece was downing a pint in one.

Whatever was to blame for the reds' failure in 1992, there is something very instructive in the response to it. Ferguson didn't blame his players, the players didn't blame him and – this is probably no coincidence – they won the title in 1993. As Mark McGhee said, the loyalty Ferguson displays to his players is exemplary. He creates a team spirit by making his players realise two things: they are all that matter and, if he can trust them, they in turn will be able to trust him absolutely. As long (as Jim Leighton will testify) as that loyalty is not in conflict with the better interests of the team. At Manchester United, an institution whose internal wranglings are of perpetual interest to the press, loyalty is proven by resisting the temptation to drop stories to the ever-listening ears.

'Nobody gets away with anything here,' Ferguson said when challenged midway through the 1993–94 season that he did not exert sufficient discipline over his sometimes wayward charges' on-field misdemeanours. 'Make no mistake about it, there's nothing wrong with a bit of discipline if it's needed and I'm not afraid to give it. [Paul McGrath would readily endorse that.] When I tell them what I think of them it is in the right place, in the privacy of the dressing-room or my office. I will never start slagging players in public. Once you do that you have lost the bolt off the dressing-room door. My job is not to criticise the players publicly. When a manager makes a public criticism, he's affecting the emotional stability of the player and that cannot be a professional thing to do.'

Though Ferguson may appear to be instinctive, there's real science in operation here, real method in his madness. Here is a man who has worked out exactly how to handle the delicate organ that is a professional footballer's ego. It is, in the end, a matter of trust. United players know their manager won't bad-mouth them in public. More than that, they know he will use what he calls his diversionary tactics to take the public heat off their misdemeanours. How many times has Ferguson, at the risk of being personally reviled, deflected media attention away from his players when they have been a little over-tasty on the pitch? Calling Jimmy Hill a prat when he, quite properly, drew attention to Cantona stamping on a Norwich player; saying the referee was mad when Peter Schmeichel was, quite legitimately, sent off in a Cup-tie against Charlton; telling the world that Dennis Wise could start a fight in a cupboard when the Chelsea player was, quite understandably, merely responding to Roy Keane. What he said to Cantona, Schmeichel and Keane in private, we will, rightly, never know.

It is also to do with honesty, something footballers respond to. Compare the manner in which Tommy Docherty got rid of Willie Morgan to the manner in which Ferguson sold Norman Whiteside. In a sense the cases were similar: two great old favourites who, the manager felt, were no longer what he wanted at the club. So Docherty initiates a whispering campaign against Morgan, agitating him beyond bearing into demanding a transfer, conduct which resulted in a court case and 21 years of bitterness. When Ferguson reached the end of his road with Whiteside, he called him into the office, didn't dither or dally about telling him he was on his way, and, after helping him wipe away his tears, gave him some advice about negotiating his new contract. No wonder Sir Richard Greenbury, boss of Marks and Spencer, is such a fan: this is the best man-manager in Britain.

It was not always thus; this is a man who has learned. Even the temper, it seems to me, has changed. From an uncontrolled blaze so intense and inarticulate the players couldn't even understand what he was on about, it has become a tool, there ready when he feels it is necessary. One senior football writer tells of standing with the press pack outside the Cliff one day and Fergie emerging and spotting a tabloid reporter, a man who had written something vaguely disparaging about United the previous week. The poor guy was subjected to the full, frightening and furious hair-dryer and sent packing, without the player interview he had arranged. The hack dispatched, barely pausing for breath, Fergie turned to the senior writer, winked and said 'how you doing, sir?' behaving as if the previous two minutes had never happened.

'I've got a temper,' Fergie once said to me. 'There's nothing wrong with losing your temper if it's for the right reasons.' And the way he smiled as he said it, you wanted to say, don't worry, mate, honestly, I won't give you cause.

'I never got the hair-dryer,' Bryan Robson told me. 'I think Fergie's said I was one of only three people he's ever worked with who hadn't – the others were Willie Miller and Eric. But I saw people who did. I was close to them at the time. And I was quite happy to remain goody-two-shoes.'

Thus, in the summer of 1995, all this suggested we should have known, should have realised, should have appreciated there was methodology at work. But we didn't. It was so hard to see the sense in what he was doing, so impossible to see the purpose. In the space of three traumatic weeks he sold Paul Ince, Andrei Kanchelskis and Mark Hughes, the guts of the 1993–94 double winners. And he bought in their place, with the £13 million he accrued from their sale? No one.

With Hughes you could, if you strained hard enough, see the logic. Time was against him, Andy Cole had been bought, he'd probably be better off spending his diminishing years in someone else's first team rather than on United's bench. But Kanchelskis, the best right winger in the world – what was going on? True, he was moaning on and on about money, but surely some accommodation could have been reached? And as for Ince, the noises he was making suggested he had been forced out, sold against his will. Ince, the best defensive midfield player in Europe (or so he told us)? You might not have gone so far as to agree with the *Manchester Evening News* poll which suggested 53 per cent of United fans thought it was time for Fergie to go, but you couldn't help thinking: has he gone bonkers, or what? Had he managed to form the club so resolutely in his own image that he now thought it didn't matter who was there as long as he was?

Such was the distress caused among United fans by Fergie's summer clear-out, that the Boss was forced to alter the habit of a lifetime and do a bit of a public relations job. He tore back from holiday in America, called a press conference, and told them his side of the story. He rang a couple of journalists he could rely on and the spin started. The message conveyed was: trust Fergie, he knows what he's doing, United will be a better team without these players.

It was difficult to see it after the first game of the 1995–96 season against Aston Villa. At half-time, wearing a dismal new outfit of John Major grey, we were lucky to be 3–0 down. No Ince, no Kanchelskis, no Hughes and with His Royal Highness King Eric still in disgrace in the stands, what was this? How could we challenge Blackburn and Liverpool by a process of asset-stripping? Never mind Newcastle who had spent £17 million over the break? It is easy to laugh at Alan Hansen now (that shouldn't necessarily stop us) but how many of us couldn't help but think he might be right on that first *Match of the Day* of the season when he reckoned 'you don't win anything with kids'?

Nine months later, when Bruce held up the Premiership trophy and Eric brandished the FA Cup, we realised what he was up to. It was April 1989 all over again, the team was being remade, never mind the pain, recast in his own image. Kanchelskis, he realised about March 1995 when the player absented himself from the season's run-in, he could never get to grips with. A man who prides himself on his ability to analyse players, Ferguson was convinced he would never work out what made the Ukranian tick (apart, of course, from large injections into the bank account). He conceded defeat, thought it best to let someone else have a go.

Ince was a different thing. In *The Diary of a Season*, his compelling account of 1994–95 written before the player was transferred, Fergie drops a couple of hints about Ince. About how he was forever missing training with a chest infection. About how he had only played three or four games all year to the level of which he was capable. It was the old commitment gap again. Ince, believing his own publicity, was full of swagger and chat, the 'guv'nor', he called himself. Fine, in Ferguson's orbit, if you are still wholly engaged in

188

the enterprise. The Boss's enterprise. I didn't think much of it at the time, but I remember, on that flight home from Barcelona, Ince was the first to break out of the despondency of defeat, to start taking the piss, to put it all into perspective. Fergie, you imagine, noticed it. And marked it.

What Ferguson admires in a player, beyond skill, balance, athleticism, is commitment to the cause. Cantona, McClair, Giggs, they've all got it. Ince, he must have thought, was losing it. Sure, he might still breathe fire in games every so often, but who was he committed to: Manchester United or Paul Ince? Fergie has a metaphor he uses about commitment. He sees it as a bus.

'I tell the players that the bus is moving on. This club has to progress. And the bus wouldn't wait for them. I tell them to get on board. Or they'll miss out. At this club we don't stop, we don't take rests, the procedure goes on and on.' Ince, he felt, was getting a bit keen on taxis; Internazionale might be the place for that sort of taste. And so it has proved.

But this still does not explain one thing: why did Ferguson not buy someone, anyone, to replace the dear departed? He didn't because he knew what we didn't know: that he could rely on the young players, Butt, Beckham, Scholes and the Neville boys. These were his kind of players, developed, nurtured, created by him in the style he demands, a style of skill and wholehearted devotion to the bus and, more particularly, its driver.

There is something romantic, appealing, Busby-esque in building a team rather than buying one. If he wanted to lay the ghost of the old man, winning the European Cup with a home-grown team is the only way to do it. But there is something Fergie-like about it too: the simple pragmatic truth that it is easier to get a young boy to grow up on your wavelength than to hope you can retune an adult newcomer. And these boys, they are on his wavelength. That's why they won him the double.

One other thing about the summer of 1995, it changed the public perception of Ferguson. As it became clear that his gamble, so incomprehensible at the time, had a steely internal logic, as it became clear he was going to win the lot again, so, in the media mind, we began to see that everything he does is calculated. After the match against Leeds in the run-in to the 1996 championship, he accused the Yorkshire players of 'cheating their manager by only trying against United'. A few unsophisticated souls read this as the kind of pitiful whining he engaged in against West Ham in 1992. But most spotted what was going on. It was a wind-up, mainly for the benefit of the Leeds players who were due to play Newcastle, his principal rivals, the following week. Poor Kevin Keegan, naïve in the wily ways of management at the top, facing for the first time all the weapons wielded by a master manipulator of the media, fell for it and, in responding, displayed his ragged, ravaged nerves for all to see. Many words were written about how Ferguson planned that one, used what little influence a manager can bring to bear from the dug-out to maximum effect. Alex Ferguson, the whinger, had become the master of psychological warfare.

I'd followed Alex Ferguson for three years, seen him in action, spoken to him at press conferences, this competitive, driven, cold-eyed man. But the longest interview I ever got with him was for the *United Family Tree* programme. He wanted to be filmed in one of the executive boxes at Old Trafford (where, I discovered as we sat around waiting for him to arrive, there are volume controls to set the noise from the plebs outside). He swept in precisely on time, sat down in the chair we had ready for him and said 'right'. That was it, no introductions, no small talk, get on with it and do it. For an hour we talked and, though polite, patient, co-operative, he gave nothing whatsoever away, told me what I had heard or read elsewhere a dozen times. Until, that is, I asked him what it was that motivated him, what it was that made him want to stay driving the bus when all destinations seemed to have been reached. He looked at me, eyes softening for a moment and said: 'The sweetest moment for me is the last minute of a victory, after that it drains away quickly. The memory's gone in half an hour, it's gone for me. It's like a drug, really, I need to re-enact it again and again to get that last-minute feeling, when you're shouting at the referee, "blow that bloody whistle."'

And I thought, yes, that's a cracker, I'll have that, that's mine. Then, two days later I was reading an interview with Sue Mott in *The Daily Telegraph* and there it was, the same quote, word for word, beat for beat. Though part of me was disappointed, I'd hoped for a connection, a little something of the great man for myself, most of me was impressed at the genius of his manipulation. With

Alex Ferguson, you see, no one ever gets more than he wants them to have.

Just one thing, though, I had to ask him now he had calmed down after the outburst at Sam, how did Fergie know we'd contacted Ralph Milne? He looked at me as if I hadn't a clue. 'Because, Ralph rang me to see if it would be all right to be interviewed.'

Ralph Milne had left the club six years prior to that phone call. And he still sought the Boss's permission. As they used to say at British Gas, don't you just love being in control?

But what finally swings it, what ultimately justifies Alex Ferguson's place in legend, is not simply that he has won more than any other manager in United history. It is that by judgement, cunning and a great big dollop of luck, he constructed the side which won the Cup final in 1994 – Schmeichel, Parker, Irwin, Bruce, Pallister, Ince, Keane, Kanchelskis, Hughes, Cantona and Giggs. This team played together only 12 times, a fleeting, sudden flowering. But they won every game they played together and won them gloriously, scoring 24 goals and conceding three. To see that team in action – Schmeichel, Parker, Pallister, Bruce and Irwin, Fort Knox solid at the back; Keane and Ince snarling and snapping and wearing the opposition down in midfield; Kanchelskis and Giggs flying; Hughes a wall to bounce passes off; and Cantona directing it all with arrogance and certainty – it wasn't just fun, it wasn't just the pleasure of triumphalism. To see them in flight was to witness football at its most elevated. It was an honour. Ferguson's creation can justifiably be reckoned United's best ever; the true dream team.